NATURAL FEELINGS, UNNATURAL ACTS

BY GERRY POSTER

VERSION 4.1

This page intentionally left blank.

NATURAL FEELINGS, UNNATURAL ACTS

FOURTH EDITION

▲ ▲

GERRY POSTER

A professional's guide to effective
persuasive communications.

Version 4.1

For more information please make contact with the author:

GERRY POSTER

- *DIRECT PHONE/FAX/VOICE MAIL 864-271-4693*
- 102 WEST MOUNTAIN VIEW AVENUE
- e-mail gerryposter@charter.net

Cataloguing-in-Publication Data

This book is available only to clients, and therefore has not been offered for Library of Congress classification. For the convenience of reference librarians, the following information is provided in like format to facilitate cataloguing.

Poster, Gerbrand III
    I. Natural Feelings, Unnatural Acts Third Edition/A professional's guide to effective persuasive communications/Gerry Poster
    196 pp + viii pp   25.5 cm x 18 cm
    "Infinite Relationships"
    ISBN 0-9724432-0-7
    1. Poster, Gerry   2. Communications   3. Persuasion
    4. Selling skills   5. Psychology of normal human relationships
    6. "Contextual communications"
    II. Title

Manufactured in the United States of America
10 9 8 7 6 5 4 3 2

LEARNING INSTITUTE PRESS
PUBLISHERS OF TRAINING MATERIALS

GREENVILLE, SOUTH CAROLINA
MOBILE, ALABAMA
AN IMPRINT OF GPA

To Gary and Karyn,
Communicators,
with love and
admiration

"Finally, beloved, whatever is true, whatever is honorable, whatever is just, whatever is pure, whatever is pleasing, whatever is commendable, if there is any excellence and if there is anything worthy of praise, think on these things."
—Paul of Tarsus

NATURAL FEELINGS, UNNATURAL ACTS

INTRODUCTION

▲   ▲

Welcome to *Natural Feelings, Unnatural Acts: A Professional's Guide to Effective Persuasive Communications*. Before we begin, there are five separate ideas we need to explore, so you will know what to expect. They are expressed in the key words of the title of this Workbook: *professional, effective, persuasive* and *communications*.

Professional is an often-misunderstood word. Originally, it meant to profess—assert—something publicly; specifically, to affirm religious faith so as to enter holy orders in the Roman Catholic (Christian) Church. Clerics (from which we also get the word *clerks*) were the only educated "professionals" in their day; all the rest (except royalty)—farmers, doctors, lawyers—were tradespeople or "practitioners." Over time, certain forms of work that required formal education came to be called "professional" as well, so today the word usually is used to indicate *any work that can be discussed—"professed"—in a formal educational setting.* Your training in your discipline makes you "professional"; by definition, so are the skills that *are "professed" here. So* this is a *professional* course *for* professionals.

Effective simply means that everything in this professional course is based on demonstrated psychological, communications and negotiation research and observation. Nothing here is theoretical or philosophical: if it's in this book, it's been proven to work in the real world, and the end result of all these methods is **action—changing another person's behavior,** so the outcomes are mutually satisfactory. The research covers over 40 years, which the present author has been studying, practicing, and teaching since 1972. However, this isn't ancient history: the most recent studies cited here were completed in late 2003.

Persuasive, as you will see in Chapter 1, is a very important word. It means to encourage or empower someone to take action or belief—to give heart and strength.

And this is done through *communications,* which means transmitting and receiving information so people can "become one"**—commune.** But, as you will learn in Chapters 3, 4, 5, 10, and 12, there is more to communication than words. Communication takes place on multiple levels simultaneously, and the effective persuasive communicator can speak on all of them.

After all this, the fifth idea—*persuasive communications* as a separate concept—may sound like an exotic or complex idea. It is neither of those— in fact, as you'll soon see, it has a familiar one-word synonym that you'll

The fundamental principle of this system is recognizing that different people approach the world in different ways, with their own personal concerns. These individual differences deserve to be respected and honored, and doing that, by understanding and accommodating other people's preferences, increases their comfort in, and willingness to coöperate with, trained communicators. This book teaches a method of making those accommodations through a practical way of *thinking about* the communication process and *responding* to individual preferences, using tools that will both reinforce and supplement things you probably already do.

Often, when discussing these tools, people become interested in *why they work.* That question requires a two-level answer.

The most obvious reason is that not only *are* we different from each other, (and at some level are *aware of those differences*), "normal" (that is "regular") people *desire to replace those differences with harmony.* And they would like to achieve that harmony by having *other people* become more like *them.* In this system we don't worry about how those differences develop; some people argue for *genetics* (the inborn patterns that shape us physically and mentally) and others argue for the power of the *environment* (the circumstances that affect us as we develop and learn how to interact with the world). The real answer probably lies between the extremes and shares input from both of them. For example, a study published in September, 2001, by researchers at the University of Connecticut, found that public school teachers were more than twice as likely to die of certain autoimmune diseases than the general population, and concluded that those teachers who had a *genetic* predisposition to the diseases were much more likely to be exposed to germs and viruses than other people because of the children they contacted in their *environment.* The two factors worked together. In the same way, in this system, we won't worry about why the human differences exist; as a persuasive communicator, you simply need to be able to *deal with them.*

The more profound reason for these tools' effectiveness is that *they satisfy deep-seated psychological needs based on a physiological component not yet fully understood.* Studies of the human brain suggest that it is a highly specialized organ, in which specific situations evoke specific responses in specific parts of the brain. For example, researchers at Stanford University reported in 2002 that the amygdala (a pea-sized part of the brain that responds to both memory and emotion when activated by certain sorts of stimuli) reacts differently in different people to such things as a smiling face. This is a *physiological* response to an *external* stimulus that generates an emotional *feeling.* In the same way, the entire brain can be understood to have physiological responses to specific stimuli, which (vastly oversimplified) can be thought of as follows.

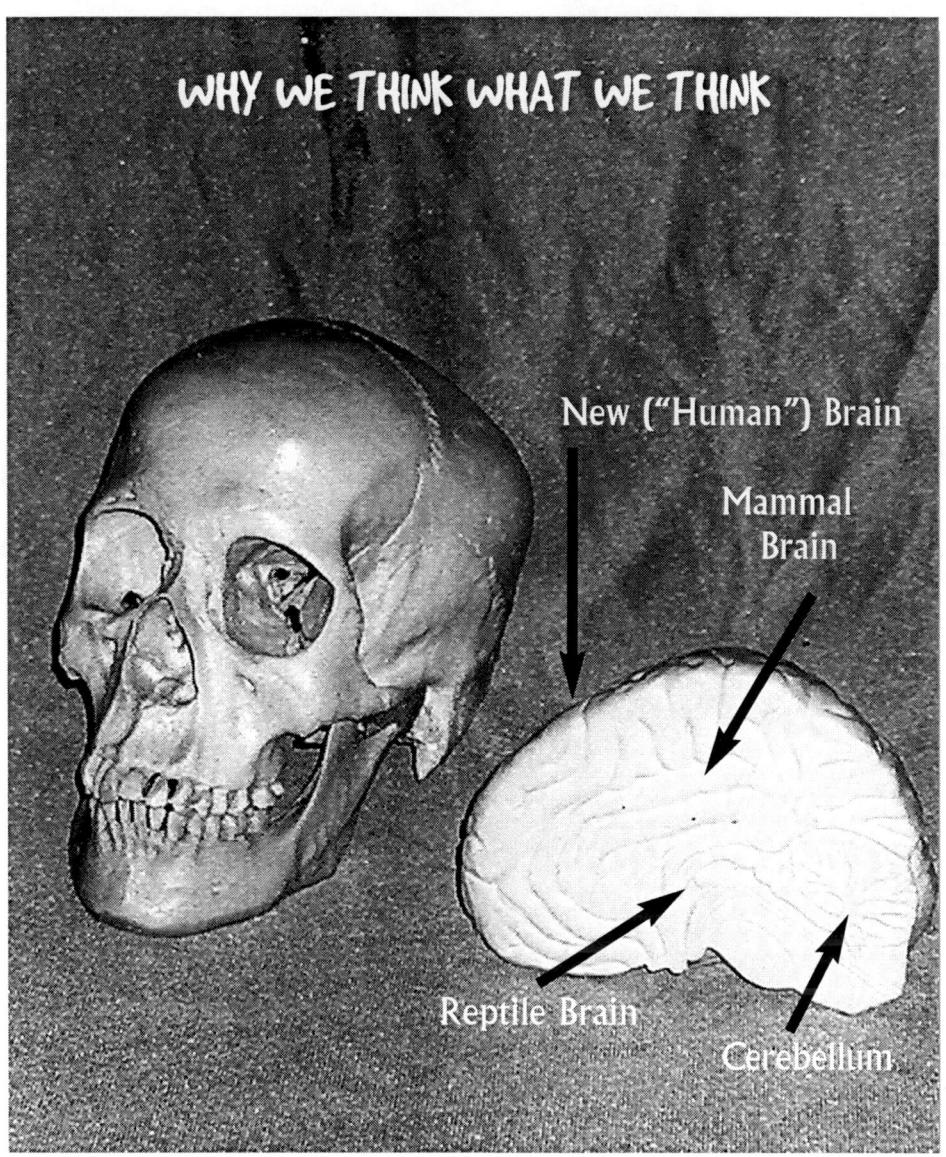

THE THREE MAIN FUNCTIONAL AREAS OF THE BRAIN

These terms are sociological, not medical. The "New Brain" processes high-er-order thoughts; the "Old (or Mammal) Brain" handles voluntary muscle movement and responses to things like color and music, and the "Reptile Brain" drives involuntary muscle motion, feelings, "intuition" and other unlearned responses. NOTE: Don't try this at home.

As the vastly oversimplified graphic on the preceding page suggests, the human brain comprises several interrelated structures, each of which performs specific tasks. The higher-order thinking that we consider "human" appears to take place on the surface of the "New Brain" (better known as the cerebrum); when exposed to such things as faces, words, or music, various areas "light up" with electrical activity as the information is apprehended and processed.

At the same time, areas deeper in the brain respond to other stimuli in equally complicated ways. For example, a small area called Broca's convolution in the left inferior frontal gyrus appear to control both *speech, mathematics* and responses to various kinds of music (and can identify "good" from "bad" music); a matching area on the right, discovered in late 2001, responds in harmony to activity in Broca's area (like a violin singing when another instrument is played nearby) and may also have similar hard-wired responses to "good" and "bad" *shape* and *color* stimuli. Other areas of this part of the brain respond to other stimuli, and drive voluntary motor actions, such as movement and facial expression. Humans and certain other higher animals share these structures, in varying degrees.

Perhaps most mysterious is the primitive area called here the "Reptile Brain," the *corpus callosum* and various glands. This part of the brain (shared with most animals above the level of sponges) controls such essential activities as breathing, heart rate, perspiration, and other still more fundamental "hard wired" responses. The important part here is the "hard wired responses" component, because they are just as *involuntary* as sweating and digesting, and are as *critical to persuasive communication* as eating is to survival. The Reptile Brain is where intuitive decisions about "liking" or "disliking" other people take place; this is where people decide whether to fight or fly when confronted with danger; this is where people fall into and out of love; this is where they decide whom to trust. This is where you want to learn to live as an effective persuasive communicator.

Here's how it works: when you move your hands, speak a sentence, or do anything else in any certain way, other people will respond to the motion or sound on three levels. Intellectually (in the "New Brain") they will process your information for content; physically (in the "Old Brain") they will prepare and execute a suitable response, *and emotionally, in the "Reptile Brain," they will decide how they feel about you*—which, in turn, will drive what seems to them to be a "suitable" response. If you want to communicate with other people, you need to learn how to generate positive responses from the Reptile Brain—which, as we have seen, seeks harmony *by ensuring that other people resemble the experiences and beliefs of its user.* And that is where this system leads you.

Why does this work? What mechanism drives this underlying method? It may be nothing more than the pleasure principle; sentient creatures naturally prefer things that cause pleasure over things that cause pain.

There are several possible ways that this might work. One physiological possibility is a variation of the *Placebo Effect*—the well-documented condition in which people's *expectations* of an effect *increase the effectiveness itself.* Howard Fields at the University of California at San Francisco, supported by new research coauthored by Fabrizio Benedetti at the University of Turin Medical School, demonstrated that the brain releases opiates when told to expect relief; this same sort of physical phenomenon may accompany the reassuring effect of affirmation received by someone with whom you use the skills you will learn here. In other words, when you employ these skills people may simply sense that you are helping them become more comfortable; from this, they may expect relief from the stresses of life, and that belief may produce the end effect of making them feel more comfortable.*

Another possibility is less exotic. It may be no more than that cannibalism and, more pointedly, murder of relatives are the exception in most animals, so we tend to associate with creatures who resemble us, believing that they represent less of a threat. Certainly, the ability to recognize kin is very well-developed among animals; recent experiments have shown that even wasps can distinguish family members from others by evaluating facial markings. By showing other people that they and we have things in common, perhaps we calm the fear of the Reptile Brain and cause mutual respect and agreement.

Still another possibility is that healthy people have a sense of social obligation and opportunity. Thus, when one person makes an effort to accommodate another, a sense of appreciation produces a sense of reciprocity, which leads to a sense of obligation.

In short, there are reasons—the roots of which are unclear, but the existence of which is demonstrable—that these tools work. It's also perfectly OK for you to be uninterested in these reasons *behind* the systems and focus instead on the *methods and outcomes* because, as noted above, *all of these tools are drawn from the real-world experiences of successful persuasive communicators, for whom they have worked and do work every day.* There is no reason why they shouldn't work for you, as well.

———

(An article in mid-2001 by Asbjørn Hróbjartsson and Peter Gøtzsche at the University of Copenhagen tried to debunk the placebo effect with statistical methods deemed by many to be suspect—but even they acknowledged that placebos relieve pain.)

Finally, now that we have discussed the keywords "professional," "effective," persuasive" and "communicative," you may be wondering about the rest of the provocative title of this handbook: *Natural Feelings, Unnatural Acts.*

As you now realize, this phrase recognizes two important facts. The first is that effective persuasive communications are based on the recognition that we should honor and respect the *natural feelings* of other people, considering those feelings as being as important as our own, and responding to them with honesty, precision, and clarity. There is nothing deceitful or manipulative in this process; indeed, quite the contrary, it is a practical expression of the dictum—common in virtually every major religion in the world—that we should do unto others as we would have them do unto us.

It is an unfortunate reality, however, that most of us do a fairly poor job of practicing this dictum in our daily lives. In fact, our regular and consistent failures to love others as we do ourselves inform many of those same major world religions—doing so is, for most people, an *unnatural act.* And therein lies the best part of this book and the systems, tools, and techniques it teaches: you can *learn* how to do these unnatural acts regularly, consistently, and powerfully. When you use them, *you* will get what you want more often; in the process you will help *others* get what *they* want (although they might not have realized what it was at first). And this book actually will help you *begin* using the skills; there are Action Activities at the end of each chapter that will convert the theories into realities, and the realities into habits. From this, you actually can make the world a better place because of your efforts.

Not a bad outcome. And although getting to that outcome will require a journey of discovery, it will be neither difficult nor dangerous. You are embarking on that journey now—enjoy the ride!

Gerry Poster

The reptile brain is so deeply entrenched in the mind that it leads people to some profound intuitions about communication. Consider these photos: on Tuesday, 2 July 2002, an alligator wandered from a creek into the Atlantic Ocean in South Carolina. In the photo above a human being named Richard Palmer of Garden City Beach, SC, is attempting to give directions to the alligator, whose name and address are unknown. The alligator appears to be striving to understand Mr. Palmer's earnest efforts, or may merely be contemplating whether or not his right hand is edible. In any case, Mr. Palmer appears convinced that communication is a reasonable possibility. The observer is not unjustified in suspecting a willed "reptile to reptile" belief on Mr. Palmer's part.

After a while, the alligator tired of the project and left. It eventually was brought to a new home, after some very careful direct intervention from the authorities.

7

"The supreme excellence is not to win a hundred victories in a hundred battles. The supreme excellence is to [obtain what you want] without even having to fight."

—Sun Tzu (alt)

NATURAL FEELINGS, UNNATURAL ACTS

CHAPTER 1: Overview
PRINCIPLES AND PRACTICE

▲   ▲

"If I always appear prepared, it is because before entering an undertaking, I have meditated long and have foreseen what might occur. It is not genius which reveals to me suddenly and secretly what I should do in circumstances unexpected by others; it is thought and preparation."
—Napoleon Bonaparte

CHAPTER 1:

▲   PRINCIPLES AND PRACTICE   ▲

This book is designed to help you develop two different skills, which are separated for the reader's convenience and ease of reference. These skills are *persuasion* and *communications.* Obviously, these are not the same things; equally obviously, they affect each other.

Persuasion usually is defined as advising, leading or encouraging someone to do something—to take a particular course of action. For its part, *communications* derives from the same root as *communism, community,* and *communion;* it means to impart, share, or *make common.* Thus, while most people think that "persuasive communications" must mean something like "talking people into something," we now realize that its true meaning is "advising people—*providing knowledge*—so they will *want to* participate in a common venture."

And this understanding changes everything. Once we stop seeing other people as objects to be manipulated, and start recognizing them as **partners in a shared enterprise,** whose interests and beliefs deserve to be *honored and respected,* we are well on our ways to becoming *effective persuasive communicators.* And we are doing so in a *professional* way, which here takes on an extra meaning: we are building professional relationships that support long-term business and social development, rather than conducting adversarial "win/lose" confrontations, in the process.

This is very important, because all social systems have two important components:
- *Individuals,* each of whom desires things for his or her own personal happiness, and
- *The group,* which has its own life and purposes (which usually includes supporting the individuals).

Notice that each of the individuals has *his or her own* desires, and these may (and often do) conflict with the goals of other individuals and/or the group. As each person tries to get his or her own sweet way, s/he quickly discovers that there are only two obvious ways of accomplishing this. These two methods can be recognized in the eternal conflict between Mom and Janet Reno.

You may remember Janet Reno, Attorney General under President Bill Clinton. When confronted with intransigent members of a religious cult in Waco, Texas, she responded by sending in tanks that set fire to the compound and killed all the members of the cult, including the children whom she was trying to protect. Similarly, when a Cuban child named Elián Gonzáles was being hidden in the home of a relative in Miami, she sent in heavily armed Federal Agents who offered the family a simple choice: death or turning over the child to the government (they chose the latter course, wisely). In these and other cases, Janet Reno achieved what she wanted through the simple expedient of using *force*. Force is an excellent way of getting what you want—as long as you can continue to apply it, because once it is removed people tend to be sullen and want to go back to their old way of doing things—the way *they* wanted. (Compare the situations in Kosovo or Israel/Palestine "before" and "after" the applications of force there.)

Then there's the other way of getting things—the way you used with your mother. Usually, you didn't have to ask for what you wanted—she just did it for you, because she *loved* you. Love has many definitions, but one that works is "The condition of feeling so strongly for another that you desire to do good things for that person."

In short, when people truly love each other, they *voluntarily* give them good things; at the other extreme, when people desire something, they can take it *by force*. These are the two simplest tools of the individual in search of happiness.

It is obvious, however, that there are serious problems with using these as methods of getting your way in a business environment, or most social situations. Pulling out a sharpened letter opener is unlikely to get the people in your supplier departments to improve their service to you; getting your boss to beat up their boss (figuratively) may help you win a battle, but you almost certainly will lose the war. Alternatively, getting everyone on the board of directors to fall in love with you may be an effective way of advancing your career, but some obvious problems with this plan show up very quickly. Clearly, another method of getting what you want is required. That method is *persuasive communications,* which can be defined as

The art and science of *making* someone *want* to do something.

Elements of both of the other, more extreme methods are present in this principle.
- First, *making* is necessary. The other person involved as your partner in this exchange by definition is unwilling to do whatever you are proposing; if not, you wouldn't have to be persuasive. Therefore, you will have to *make* him or her take action.
- But you must make him or her *want* what you are proposing, because you can't force *the outcome.* You will have to *communicate* the benefits of the outcome, and make the other person happy that you did it.
- This process can be called by another, simpler name: *selling.* In fact, *selling* (once understood) can be seen to be the glue that holds society together.

But this glue needs to be examined more closely. It is not without its hazards: the ability to **make** someone want to do something can harm or destroy the relationship if the **outcome** is bad. Consider, for example, Adolf Hitler, David Koresh, or John Allen Muhammad (the Virginia/Maryland sniper)—each was elected or selected by one or more willing followers who were found to be in dire straits (or worse) when the end came. Since the goal of Effective Persuasive Communicators is **infinite relationships,** we must modify the definition of persuasive communications to read:

The art and science of making someone want to do something that he or she needs.

Now it is truly effective, truly ethical and truly **worthwhile** communication.

Which leads to the next point. As noted above, "communications" means to impart, share, or *make common.* Words are excellent methods of communication, but not the only tools available. Anyone who has ever winked at someone else, sent a drink to someone at another table in a restaurant, intentionally put a stamp upside down on a letter or performed any of thousands of other "non-verbal" communications, knows that words are not the only way of transmitting information. In fact, they may not even be the *best* way of "saying" something: in study after study, when people receive conflicting messages from another person—one through words, and another through "body language"—the *non-verbal* message (the one received by the "Reptile Brain") is trusted more often than the verbal one received by the rational "word-processor" parts of the brain.

How does all this fit into the fabric of professional relationships? As one of the three points of the interpersonal triangle. Relationships—especially those in professional environments—usually are in one of three roles:
- Leader/Follower (Team Member)
- Teacher/Student
- Seller (Motivator)/Buyer.

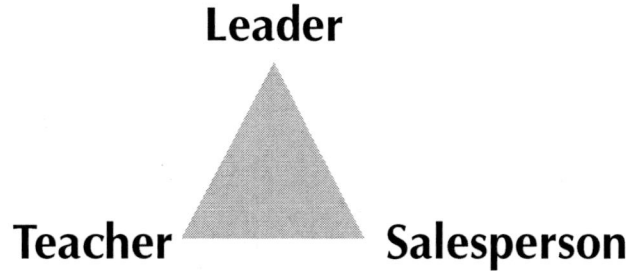

Leader

Teacher   **Salesperson**

A *Teacher* is someone who provides (ideally relevant and useful) information to someone else; in order to make the information relevant and useful, the teacher must *learn* about the desires of the other person.

A *Leader* is someone who has a *follower* and is going someplace. This requires knowledge both of methods of leadership and of mutually desirable destinations.

A *Salesperson* is someone who can get another person to take action, usually involving changing behaviors in response to a *product.* The product does not have to be a tangible thing; it could be the "product of a discussion": a changed belief, a commitment, or a shared outlook—but it does require the other person (the "customer") to give up something as a form of "payment." It could be money, time, personal freedom, or any of many other things that people value.

Finally, all this requires that we recognize that our partner in this venture (the customer) has specific roles as well, each of which must be respected and honored.

The *"Student"* deserves to be talked "to" and "with," not "down to" or "at." This is essential if you are to teach.

Your partner will be a *"Follower"* only if she or he perceives that the journey will be personally beneficial. Therefore, *his or her needs* must be honored. And the honoring and respect must include recognition of both his or her *physical* needs (that are satisfied by the product) and *psychic* needs (that are satisfied by the way the product is presented).

The *"Customer"* will "buy" only when she or he is convinced that the product is worth what it costs. This cost/benefit analysis is performed subjectively and continually, evaluating each type of "payment" suggested above: psychic comfort, convenience, personal trade-offs in freedom and resources, and so on.

These three are parts of the whole of relationships, and these are the roles the professional must be able to doff and don as required by circumstance—sometimes wearing two or three hats at once. As you do it, keep in mind that you *are* changing roles, and that you are having to *work* at being an effective communicator—and that it all is based on *honoring* and *respecting the other person.*

This is not difficult to learn, although it comes more naturally to some people than to others. The people we call "Natural-born Salespeople" have it, as do many religious leaders. But there are many salespeople, ministers, and business leaders who were *not* "born" into their talents, and yet they have triumphed. That's because even though certain things come *easier* to certain people than to others, *anyone* can learn how to *improve* a skill. Someone 7' 8" tall probably will have natural advantages at basketball, but that doesn't mean that a really hard-working 5' 10" player can't get *better.* Selling is a gift, but—*like any other profession*—it also is a *transferable skill,* because it can be quantified and learned.

Here, you will learn three distinct types of transferable skills. The first is the skill of understanding the circumstance in which you are working. You will learn how to analyze
- Yourself,
- Your "Product" (the desired outcome of your persuasion), and
- The available opportunities in the needs of the person with whom you are partnering.

The second set of skills you will learn deal with *verbal and non-verbal communication* tools, broken into five components:
- Understanding how individual people *provide* information, so you can gather information about their needs and provide benefits;
- Discovering how people *acquire* information, so you can present your ideas to maximize their perception and acceptance;
- Identifying how they *process* information, to provide the level of detail and intellectual framework that makes them most comfortable,
- Determining how they *relate to authority,* to meet their psychological expectations *one-on-one, with you as a person,* and
- Realizing how they *make decisions,* so you can bring them to a conclusion efficiently and comfortably.

Third, you will learn how to use the three-step planning model so that you can place the *communication* skills into the context of a *persuasive* (that is, results-oriented) outcome. The steps are:
- How to set attainable goals,
- How to build win/win positions in your goals, and
- How to anticipate and prevent normal abnormalities.

In each of these studies you will develop strategies and systems for *yourself,* as an individual, through both readings and exercises.

Finally, you will learn some skills for handling the unexpected—the events that, occurring spontaneously, alter and illuminate our times. Remembering that if everything went right, there would be no adventures, you will acquire specific responses to make the adventures more like fun and less like calamity. Again, there will be Action Plans to make this more useful.

So—if you are ready—please reflect, make a temporary peace with any suspicions or philosophical disagreements you have, and let's start.

"Only reason can convince us of those three fundamental truths without a recognition of which there can be no effective liberty:
—that which we believe is not necessarily true;
—that what we like is not necessarily good, and
—that all questions are open."

—Clive Bell (alt)

Chapter 1
Action Activity

There are many kinds of knowledge. There is factual knowledge, such as the data recalled by savants and computers. There is intellectual knowledge, such as the wisdom of professors and philosophers. There is practical knowledge, such as the mechanical skills of surgeons and plumbers. And there is *muscle knowledge*—the understanding of *how to do important things correctly and repeatedly* that distinguishes the great athletes, communicators, and leaders of the ages. These people know how to "do the right thing" without having to think about it, *because they have done the same things in practice countless times.* The situation that stymies an amateur when encountered in competition is a breeze for the professional with muscle memory, because she or he has done it hundreds of times before, *without the pressure of having to figure out a solution,* and knows what to do "intuitively." Please reread the quotation from Napoleon at the beginning of this chapter.

But we don't have to go as far back as Napoleon to find a examples of this. Try golf: Tiger Woods often is asked what gifts make him such a great "Natural golfer." His reply always is the same: "Anyone can be as good a golfer as I am. They only have to hit 1000 golf balls every day from the time they are 4 years old." In college, Woods was famous for going out to practice on days that his teammates rested because of bad weather: in windstorms, heat waves, driving rain, he hit 1000 golf balls a day. The pro tour has few surprises for him.

Or try crafts: Martha Stewart, like her or hate her, has built an empire single-handedly. Her relentless pursuit of perfection and careful attention to detail have been the source of several highly critical articles and books. But whatever else can be said, she has practiced her craft diligently and remained true to its demands: when under attack for questionable stock trading, she said "I'm going to focus on my salads."

Or try cycling. Lance Armstrong, the amazing American who came back from testicular cancer to win the *Tour de France* four times, freely admits that it was the destruction of his natural gifts by chemotherapy and other disciplines that taught him to work at his craft. Cynics refuse to believe that he can be so good without being on drugs, to which Armstrong replies (in a Nike ad quoted in the July 15, 2002, *New Yorker*) "Everybody wants to know what I'm on. What am I on? I'm on my bike, busting my [behind] six hours a day. What are you on?"

Which brings us to the subject of these Action Activities.

If you want to learn about the principles of effective persuasive communication, you can read this book (or any of the hundreds of other, similar books on leading, selling, communicating, managing, guiding, healing, parenting, or motivating). The truth of it is, most of these books teach most of the same things, for the simple reason that these skills are true and they work. If you read this, or any of the others, you will have intellectual knowledge about the subject.

But if you want to *be* an Effective Persuasive Communicator who can work *with* Professionals, you will have to do more. You will have to *become* a professional in these *skills.* And that means you will have to hit some golf balls, make some salad, or get on your bike. In that way, you can build the *muscle memory* that will make you a successful effective professional persuasive communicator. The opportunity to do that lies in these Action Activities, because they convert the *knowledge* in these pages into *practical work skills* you can take back to the job. They are sequential, meaning that you need to start with the steps here in Chapter 1; by the time you get to the end, you will have practiced them all and can continue your practice in the real world.

These Activities are divided into two parts. The first part is a *General Activity,* which allows you to think about the people and events in the world in which you work globally and develop large-scale strategies for dealing with them. These are intentionally *open-ended* so you can decide how far to take the exercises to meet your needs.

The second part is always a *specific Activity.* These focus on a single real-world task in which you are engaged, so you can apply the skills to a small-scale test track and see how they work. These are intentionally *repetitive,* so you can follow the sequence several times as you perfect your skills.

Will these make you a great communicator? Will you be as good at persuading people as Tiger Woods is at golf, Martha Stewart is at domesticity, Lance Armstrong is at cycling, or any of them is at making money? If you have it in you, yes; if not, if your "natural" talents aren't as focused on one thing as they are, you will merely be **much more successful than you could have been otherwise.** In other words, the least you can expect is being much better than you are right now, and the best you can hope for is superstardom. The only *sure* promise is that you if you do *nothing* you know *exactly* how much improvement you will enjoy. There's little to lose, and lots to gain— grab for it!

General Activity

The first step in building a long-range action plan is assembling lists of your assets, resources and liabilities. The most important asset is, of course, the people with whom you work and the relationship you have with each of them. ***Please notice that all types of relationships should be considered; you need the same effective persuasive communication skills for teammates, supervisors, or subordinates.*** Please complete this simple survey:

To "rate the quality of the relationship" use a word ("Good," "Poor," "Wonderful," or the like), or a letter grade, such as "A," "C," "F" or the like.

Answer "What is your usual role" with one or more of these words: "Leader," "Follower," "Teacher," "Student, "Seller (Motivator)" or "Buyer."

Describe the tools used with words such as "Suggestion/agreement," "Force," "Partnering," "Discussion," "Trickery," or the like. Be honest.

PERSON	RELATIONSHIP	Rate the *quality* of your relationship	What is your *usual role* in the relationship?	What *tools* usually are used in this relationship to cause change?
_____	_____	_____	_____	_____
_____	_____	_____	_____	_____
_____	_____	_____	_____	_____
_____	_____	_____	_____	_____
_____	_____	_____	_____	_____
_____	_____	_____	_____	_____
_____	_____	_____	_____	_____
_____	_____	_____	_____	_____
_____	_____	_____	_____	_____

You have a life outside the office, of course, and it should be at least as important to you as your business world. The skills you are learning here also will work in these personal and social lives. Please repeat the assessment you made on the previous page, using the same standards and systems.

Your PERSONAL life (Family, close friends)

PERSON	RELATIONSHIP	Rate the *quality* of your relationship	What is your *usual role* in the relationship?	What *tools* usually are used in this relationship to cause change?
————	————	————	————	————
————	————	————	————	————
————	————	————	————	————
————	————	————	————	————
————	————	————	————	————
————	————	————	————	————

Your SOCIAL life (Friends, clubs, worship circles)

PERSON	RELATIONSHIP	QUALITY	YOUR ROLE	USUAL TOOLS
————	————	————	————	————
————	————	————	————	————
————	————	————	————	————
————	————	————	————	————
————	————	————	————	————
————	————	————	————	————

If necessary, you can continue this exercise on regular paper, of course.

Specific Activity

Select a current or upcoming project of reasonable importance to your and your group's success, which will require you to work with one or more people. They can be people identified in the General Activity, or different people. Please *very thoughtfully* complete the following preliminary analysis:

The Project: _____

_____

The Desired Outcome:_____

_____

The People with whom I shall have to work:

Person 1: *Name* _____ *Relationship* _____

Predictable problems when it comes to achieving a harmonious working relationship and reaching a mutually acceptable resolution with him/her:

_____

_____

My best guess why these problems occur: _____

_____

Person 2: *Name* _____ *Relationship* _____

Predictable problems when it comes to achieving a harmonious working relationship and reaching a mutually acceptable resolution with him/her:

_____

_____

My best guess why these problems occur: _____

_____

Did you phrase the "best guesses" in words that honor the other people? Please continue on the next page.

Person 3: *Name* _____ *Relationship* _____

Predictable problems when it comes to achieving a harmonious working relationship and reaching a mutually acceptable resolution with him/her:

_____

_____

My best guess why these problems occur: _____

_____

Person 4: *Name* _____ *Relationship* _____

Predictable problems when it comes to achieving a harmonious working relationship and reaching a mutually acceptable resolution with him/her:

_____

_____

My best guess why these problems occur: _____

_____

Person 5: *Name* _____ *Relationship* _____

Predictable problems when it comes to achieving a harmonious working relationship and reaching a mutually acceptable resolution with him/her:

_____

_____

My best guess why these problems occur: _____

_____

Person 6: *Name* _____ *Relationship* _____

Predictable problems when it comes to achieving a harmonious working relationship and reaching a mutually acceptable resolution with him/her:

_____

_____

My best guess why these problems occur: _____

_____

Did you phrase the "best guesses" in words that honor the other people?

CHAPTER 2: THE THREE PKS

▲   MIBU, WIIFMS, AND "SO WHAT?"   ▲

"The customer is never wrong." ("*Le client n'a jamais tort.*")

—Cesar Ritz

As we have seen, there are two steps in persuasive communication: *communicating,* and *persuading.* The sequence, obviously, must be first to communicate, and then to persuade; even Janet Reno's Justice Department's assault rifles were tools for *communicating* the Agent's willingness to kill before they could be *persuasive.* The same model must be used in the workplace: first, make sure you are using the correct method of communicating; then, set about persuading.

That sounds obvious, and it is—but no less important because it is obvious. And notice that in this example the *communication* was accomplished without *words*—the *weapons* carried by the Agents sent the message about the government's intent. But this message worked only because Gonzáles' family *recognized what the weapons were.* If the Justice Department Agent had pointed an exotic weapon resembling a sunflower at Donato Dalrymple (the fisherman holding the little boy) there would have been no communication, and therefore no persuasion.

This breakdown occurs often in attempted persuasion. The speaker uses language *he or she likes,* rather than the language of the person *with whom s/he is trying to communicate.* Consider the example in the preceding paragraph: if the reader is a fan of Janet Reno, the point of the present argument will be obscured because the *writer's words do not match the reader's intellectual vocabulary*.*

Please notice that when such a breakdown between would-be persuader and sought-after partner occurs, the communicator's usual response is to overcome it by using more words. The problem with this is obvious: if the speaker continues to use the same words, they not only will not improve the situation, but also they may even make it worse, by rubbing more salt into an open wound; in this case, an offended reader would not be mollified by *more* examples that vilified Janet Reno. Instead, the smart communicator will *change tactics,* modify his or her verbal (and intellectual) vocabulary, and try again. To repeat: failure to use the language of the listener is as useless as trying to get directions to a hotel by speaking English to a French-speaking shopkeeper. No number of words, at any level of volume, will have any effect on the situation. You may wind up sleeping under the stars unless you use the language of the shopkeeper. In the same way, you must identify the language needs of your partner before you try to be a persuasive communicator.

------

*The Present Writer apologizes to any offended Gentle Readers, and hopes they will understand that this was a pedagogical tool and move forward.

Of course, at this point you may be thinking, "But the parallel doesn't hold. In my work, I deal with people who speak the same language as I do—there is no barrier among English-speaking workers." The sad answer is that, while the *verbal* language may be the same, this is only part of the story. *Many* languages—gesture, tone of voice, body language, and more—are at work, and they (*as well as* the verbal language) can be *very* different.

Books have been written about communications idiosyncrasies. There are differences between the expectations of men and women, Europeans and non-Europeans, various generations of people in a given culture, and more. These are books about *languages,* and how they influence *communication.* Here, we will not try to *analyze* other people's languages, because that takes far too long. Instead, we will discover how to *speak* those languages quickly and effectively; as noted in the previous Chapter, this will take place at several levels, and cover a lot of ground. But all of it has the same goal: enhancing communications.

The first step in doing this is returning to our definition of effective persuasive communication (*aka* "selling"), which is that it is **The Art and Science of Making Someone Want Something that She or He Needs.** There are several languages at work when people talk about changing behaviors or choosing a course of action ("Making someone want to do something that she or he needs.") One of them is the fact that ***my reasons for wanting something*** *might not be the same as yours.* My opinion of working on weekends, blue, fountain pens or Volvos may be so different from yours that any attempt we make to discuss them will be blocked by our opinions; my expectations about what makes a "Good employee" or describes an "Ideal car" may be so different from yours that we literally "don't speak the same language." Let's explore this in more detail.

And, as we do so, let's start with at least *one* a clear shared belief and conviction. Nothing discussed in this book is about misusing or misleading people. That is not "Effective persuasive communication"; it is called "Deception and deceit." Any decent, human approach to other people must be based on *honoring and respecting* them, making their concerns as important to you as your own. If you do not choose to do this, please leave now.

A second important belief we must share is that persuading people whom you honor and respect is possible only when you *understand* them. Most of this book is about learning how to understand people so you can honor and respect them and their needs, and an essential first step in doing that is learning who the other person is, so we can speak their motivational, linguistic, kinesic and sociological languages. This can take place only when we understand the concept of self-perception.

To a greater or lesser degree, each of us is convinced, somewhere deep inside, that *we* are the model God had in mind when the world was created*. *Our* tastes and preferences define "excellence"; *our* country or football team is the best; *our* religion has the right answers. We are, in a word, **MIBU**™—the **M**ost **I**mportant **B**eing in the **U**niverse. Most people can keep this conviction under control (when it goes out of control the resulting afflictions are called *solipsism* as a philosophical condition or *autism* as a medical one); however, it is always there (except in saints). *Overcoming* it in day-to-day behavior without denying it as a part of one's own natural make-up (as you are about to learn how to do) is a sign of intelligence and mental health.

Are people wrong in believing they are MIBU? Not in a biological sense. If and when you cease to exist, the universe, as far as you care, will cease to exist as well; you may as well be MIBU (as long as I can be, too). Even if you aren't MIBU, we'll get along better if I *assume* you are.

Which leads to the third key concept, which obviously must be *want.* A "want" is a lack; "wanting" is desiring to fill the gap made by the lack. Effective Persuasive Communication starts by finding out the precise shape of a hole in MIBU's heart and then providing something that will fill the hole as close to perfectly as we can manage, in a way that makes the other person realize that we know they are MIBU. The task is complicated by the fact that many people are unaware that they *have* a hole in their hearts, or know it's there but not what it's shaped like. These are manageable problems, which are handled later in this handbook. For now, let's focus on the hole itself.

The hole can be almost anything. As communicators, rather than psychoanalysts, our goal is to *fill* rather than *heal* it. The first step is naming it, and for this we'll use a familiar term, based on looking at a *desired outcome* from *another person's point of view:* **WIIFM** (pronounced *"wiff-em"*); the letters stand for the question "**W**hat's **i**n **i**t **f**or **me**?"

Where do WIIFMS come from? From *Products,* of course. (Remember, a "Product" is the outcome of a persuasive communication exchange. It can be tangible, such as a car, or intangible, such as agreeing to cooperate on a task. Both are "products" of communication.) WIIFMS come in all shapes, sizes, flavors, and colors, and many seem incomprehensibly stupid to other people. That's one of the two great things about WIIFMS: you don't have to agree with or even understand them. You merely have to know what they are. (The other great thing about WIIFMS is that they *are* different—otherwise, we'd all be chasing after the same people, cars, clothes, and so on.)

Or nature was constructed to select when the species evolved; *your choice.*

27

All of this leads to the 3 PK Model of Persuasive Communication. There are three types of Knowledge required in any attempt to modify another person's behavior: knowledge of the other *person,* knowledge of the *tools* used for communication, and a proper understanding of the *product,* as viewed from MIBU's perspective. It looks like this:

$$PK_1 : PRODUCT\ KNOWLEDGE$$

| PK_2: | PK_3: |
| PEOPLE KNOWLEDGE | PROCESS KNOWLEDGE |

Obviously, then, if you want to be an effective persuasive communicator the first step will have to be understanding the product you have to sell—that is, the outcome you desire to achieve. You must know more about the product than anyone else, because that is how you will earn the right to persuade the other person to accept your recommendation. This is PK_1 "Product Knowledge." However, remember that PK_1 is just *one* of *three* kinds of knowledge owned by effective persuasive communicators. The others are knowledge of the *People* involved in the partnership, and the *Process* of effective persuasive communication. These are three elements in effective persuasive communication—three "PK's":

- PK_1—**Product Knowledge.** You must decide carefully what you have to "sell," and understand it in terms of the *needs* of the *people.* You are responsible for this; no one else can or will take the time to do this essential step. You will practice it in this chapter's Action Step.

- PK_2—**People Knowledge.** You use specific skills to gather this information, which we'll discuss in the next chapter; you began the process in the preceding one, where you identified the people with whom you work on projects generally and specifically.

- PK_3—**Process Knowledge.** You are acquiring knowledge in the process skills of persuasive communication right now; the rest of this book describes them in greater detail, And you have made the first leap simply by reading this far: you have accepted and built on the recognition that all people are different. Just as different MIBUS have different *WIIFMS,* they also have different *psychological* and *communications* needs.

Of course, most people don't make an effort to discover the WIIFMs of other MIBUs. That's why there are so few good communicators in the world. The really *powerful* communicators—sociopaths, politicians, con men and other undesirables—are effective precisely *because* they "feel our pain"—or *can convince us to believe they do.* In short, these communicators' PK_1 Product Knowledge is far less important to their success than the fact that they understand individuals' desires—what we are calling *People Knowledge.*

You can learn how to uncover People Knowledge *without* becoming a threat to society; the great leaders of religious history—Jesus, Mohammed, K'ung Ch'iu, Gautama, and so on—also knew how to fill the greatest WIIFM need of all, even though Jim Jones did, too. The *tools* of persuasive communication are powerful; the user determines how they are *used.*

Again, PK_2 isn't difficult. You only have to remember that each distinguishing characteristic of the product (the goal of your persuasive communication) can be viewed in either of two ways: what it *is* (which is a *feature* that describes it), or what it *does* for another person (which is a feature combined with a *need,* equaling a *benefit*).

This very simple realization is profoundly powerful. A seat belt in a car is a *feature,* and it costs the manufacturer about $15 to make and install it. Deleting seat belts from cars would reduce their cost by about $75. If you were to ask the average prospective buyer if she or he would like to save $75 by eliminating some nylon and metal, you probably would get a "Yes" answer, but once the buyer realized you were going to remove something that could prevent or reduce death or injuries in an accident—seat belts—his or her attitude probably would change. When you described the object as a bit of material, it was a *feature* and properly perceived as being suspect. But when you described *what it could do for the user,* it became a *benefit.* Here are a few more examples:

FEATURES	BENEFITS
Plastic insert for your shoes.	Relieve leg pain and improve posture.
"Fuzzy logic" laser-reader.	CD players you can play while jogging.
Fluorocarbon layer on steel.	Pan that cleans easily—"Teflon®"
CO monitors on auto exhaust.	Clean air and easier breathing.
Nylon with longitudinal holes.	Carpet fiber that doesn't show dirt.

You get the idea: simply by honoring the other person, and considering his or her ideas and concerns as important as our own—recognizing that she or he is MIBU, in other words—allows us to think about what we want to recommend (our product) in a new light. And this light allows the other person to see what we want to display for consideration.

The same principle works if we are trying to convince another person in an office situation. For example, suppose that you want to persuade another person to select a cutting-edge color for a project, and the other person prefers a safe, neutral beige. Your *product* is getting the color you prefer specified. If you describe it in terms of its *features,* you are unlikely to get anywhere. For example, here's a statement by a designer: "This is a really neat color. It's showing up in the color forecasts, and we're seeing it in fashion fabrics already. I love it!"

This is all about the designer, and not at all about the other person. Here are the same features converted into benefits. This is done simply by assuming you are the other person, and speaking about *his or her needs* instead of your own.

FEATURES	BENEFITS
This is a really neat color.	This is a safe and secure choice. People will admire it.
It's showing up in the color forecasts.	You will get long use from this color, because it is ahead of the trends
We're seeing it in fashion fabrics already.	It will be easy to select furnishings, now and in the future.
I love it!	You can be trust this selection, since the pro you hired has confidence in it.

Now, compare these two sentences and see which *you* would find more convincing and persuasive:

"This is a really neat color. It's showing up in the color forecasts, and we're seeing it in fashion fabrics already. I love it!"

"If you select this color, people will admire your good taste. This is a safe and secure choice. You will get long use from this color, because it is ahead of the trends. It will be easy to select furnishings, now and in the future. You can be trust this selection, since the pro you hired has confidence in it."

It should be obvious: the first paragraph is about me, and you are less interested in me than you are in yourself. And the second is about MIBU, and you are much more likely to pay attention and be convinced.

Obviously, you must understand the other person in order to convert features into benefits. And it does take effort; after all, this is a most "Unnatural act." Yet while it is unnatural, it is not impossible (nor even difficult, once you get used to it). All you have to do is go back to the concept of the WIIFM and ask yourself, "What are the possible holes in MIBU's heart that I could fill with this product? What, in short, are some *needs* that I can support with this recommendation?"

In the example above, we assumed (from the fact that the other person was planning to go with a neutral beige) that she or he felt a need for safety and security. Thus, all the benefits focused on that sort of need. If, on the other hand, the other person was teetering between two wild color possibilities, and the designer were recommending one on the basis of a better æsthetic, then the benefits might have been quite different. It might have gone like this:

FEATURES	BENEFITS
This is a really neat color.	Stylists feel this color will give your project the look you are trying to achieve.
It's showing up in the color forecasts.	It is out on the cutting edge, and will demonstrate your fashion sense.
We're seeing it in fashion fabrics already.	Other designers agree this is going to be a very trendy choice.
I love it!	As a fellow professional, I am willing to put my signature on this with you.

By matching the need to the feature, you can produce benefits; from this, you can begin the task of convincing. Whenever there is a need, there is the prospect of a benefit; where there is no need, there is no benefit, and the feature is never brought up to the other person in the conversation.

This means that the first task of the effective persuasive communicator must be examining all the possible "products" she or he has to "sell," and imagining as many needs as possible in order to convert features into benefits. Or, if you have only a single thing to propose or sell—such as a decision or selection of a single item—you need only to determine as many *possible needs* for as many *possible MIBUs* as you can imagine in order to be prepared for whatever needs it turns out each has.

But how do you do this? Is there any sort of formula or system that will make the conversion possible? Luckily, yes; all you have to do is ask two rude questions about each feature, which are

"So what?"

This question, asked repeatedly about each possible feature, will tell you how to convert the feature into a benefit. In other words, answering the PK_3 question "So what?" forces you to think about the various possible *human applications* of these PK_1 *features.* Then, by asking the second question—

"Who cares?"

you uncover specific possible PK_2 *people* for whom the PK_1 features will be benefits. Thus prepared, you can go out and search for specific individuals to whom you can provide help, support, and *benefits.* You can then introduce the WIIFMS to your partner in a supportive, non-confrontational way.

Of course, a given feature can have many different benefits, depending on various MIBU's needs. You need to know as many as possible, to be prepared for the greatest possible number of people. Each of them can be identified by asking "So what?" and "Who cares?" often enough.

For example, suppose you are trying persuade someone to put a squirrel shield on the backyard bird feeder. You recommend a slippery rounded plastic disc, loosely hung above the feeder, so that squirrels will be unable to climb down the rope to the feeder and get the birdseed.

FEATURE	"SO WHAT?"	"WHO CARES?"
Slippery rounded plastic disc, loosely hung above the bird feeder.	Squirrels will slip off.	Someone who wants to leave the bird seed for the birds.
	Squirrels won't be poisoned or hurt.	Someone who likes squirrels.
	Simple, cheap, easy to install.	Someone with little mechanical ability.
	Side benefit: will keep seed dry if it rains.	Someone who doesn't like messing with feeder.

Now let's apply this to the office. Assume that your goal is to convince somebody to work 6 hours over the weekend in order to process a big order that came in late Friday, and needs to ship Monday afternoon by 5:00 PM. Only one person—Kelly Jones—has the skill and expertise required. You are prepared to reward Kelly with double time off and a bonus in exchange for the help, but you aren't certain if those will be attractive compensation. You plan for the conversation as follows:

FEATURE (Characteristics of your product.)	"SO WHAT?" (What could these do?)	"WHO CARES?" (Describe someone who might find this good.)
1. Chance to help close a big sale.	Ensure company's profitability.	Someone who wants job security.
	Make bonuses possible later on.	Someone with kids or other gift needs.
	Give employees a psychological boost.	Someone who cared for other people.
2. Extra time off at a later date.	Give personal control for time off.	Someone with personal needs.
		Someone who wants to control his/her destiny.
	Have greater amount of free time.	Someone with hobby, family, tasks.
	Allow free time in the middle of week.	Someone with kids in school programs.
		Someone who like baseball games.
		Someone who wants to do his/her "own thing."
3. Extra pay.	Can buy something special for self.	Someone with hobby or other interest.
	Can buy gifts for others.	Someone who knows holidays come.

Notice that a single feature can lead to several different WIIFMS.

And now you are prepared for your conversation with Kelly. Instead of asking, "Kelly, how'd you like to work all weekend?"—to which the only sensible answer (unless one had only a horrible alternative, such as a miserable home life) would be a moaned "Please, boss, not me!"—you will ask one or more of the following questions:

(If Kelly is concerned about job security):

"Kelly, would you be willing to help me ensure our Company's long-term profitability and job security?"

(If Kelly has children or other people for whom gift-buying is important):

"Kelly, would you be willing to help me increase the likelihood of our having extra money for Holiday bonuses this year?"

(If Kelly cares about the Company and co-workers):

"Kelly, would you be willing to help me make a big psychological boost for the Company and its people?"

(If Kelly wants to be able to take time off whenever wanted):

"Kelly, would you like to get a little credit in the time clock, so you could take off whenever you needed to later on?"

(If Kelly is an independent, free-thinking soul):

"Kelly, how'd you like to be able to take some time off whenever you darned well felt like it?"

(If Kelly's hobby, family, or interests make mid-week free time desirable):

"Kelly, how'd you like a little extra time off to [spend with your model trains] [be with your family] [go to your kids' school programs] [take in a mid-week double header] [spend some time on your own]?"

(If Kelly could use a little extra money for something special):

"Kelly, how'd you like to get a little free money to spend on your [model trains] [family at the Holidays] [anything else **specific**]?"

You get the idea. Convert the *feature* into a **specific** *benefit* by asking "So What?" and "Who cares?" and your WIIFMS will help you think like MIBU—and that will help you get what's good for *both* of you.

Two things are immediately obvious. The first is that an effective persuasive communicator must begin by developing as many *benefits* as possible, to meet as many potential *needs* as possible with legitimate *features* of the PK$_1$ "product." Failure to take the time to prepare will almost certainly result in speaking the wrong "language" of the other person's needs, and surely communicate a lack of respect and honor for that person at the same time.

And equally obviously, the more PK$_2$ People Knowledge we have, the better our chances of being persuasive—*if we **also** have the right Product Knowledge to match those people's needs and desires (provide WIIFMS to MIBU) with characteristics of whatever we are recommending.*

If you know only *two* details about whatever you want to recommend to your communications partner—how it looks, or something it can do—you can match them to the holes in your partner's heart and produce WIIFMS. *But you know **ten** things about it, you have **five times better** a chance of filling the hole in the person's heart, or filling five times as many holes. If you know **twenty** things, your chances of success double again.*

This reveals the two parts of a WIIFM: you must know both what the other person *desires and* what you have available to *meet* that desire. That requires you to understand your proposal completely and thoroughly. Until you do, you can't dance and sing with the music your partner wants to hear.

So, how are you going to *discover* the needs and desires of your partner (PK$_2$ People Knowledge) in order to match them to your carefully prepared PK$_1$ Product Knowledge? By reading the next chapter and mastering a few simple PK$_3$ *Process Knowledge* skills for discovery, analysis, and rapport-building that complete the cycle of persuasive communication. Once you know these processes, you can use them both to understand and convince people about your product, and be an effective persuasive communicator. Thus, there are two parts to this strategy of persuasive communication:

- The **hard step:** the skills of converting features into benefits with WIIFMS and matching the right WIIFMS with each individual person's needs, and
- The **soft step:** the skills of matching communications strategies to each person with whom we deal.

Obviously, the soft stuff is the hard stuff; we'll study that next.

Chapter 2
Action Activity

There are two equal and matched skills required: establishing an understanding of the world in which we live (which helps define *its* PK_2 parameters), and building a sense of PK_1—the **product** we are bringing to the table. "Product" means more than "a thing being sold"—since all normal human communication relies on persuasion, "product" is the desired outcome of the sales conversation. Reflecting on the *people* will help you decide whether or not it is even possible to proceed with the persuasion—and, if you decide it is feasible, what to make the product look like. (This is part of, but not the same as, *establishing goals,* which is handled in detail in a later step of this PK_3 Process.)

General Activity

What is your general responsibility for the real world PK_2 people listed in Action Step 1? In other words, what are you responsible for "selling" to them—daily actions? Attitudes, toward the organization or their Associates? A specific behavior? Once you have identified the *product,* can you quantify or measure it—for example, if you are responsible for people's attitudes toward their work, can this be measured by scores on satisfaction surveys, production output, or actions at work, or something else?

Key things for which I am responsible: *How to measure success:*

1. _____   _____
   _____   _____

2. _____   _____
   _____   _____

3. _____   _____
   _____   _____

4. _____   _____
   _____   _____

5. _____   _____
   _____   _____

6. _____   _____
   _____   _____

Specific Activity

Return to the current or upcoming project you identified in the Action Activity for Chapter 1. List that specific *product* here—the intended outcome of your persuasive efforts, to which you must convince the other people to agree. This should be a simple sentence, such as "I must convince them to continue working under undesirable conditions [such as the absence of raises]," or "I must convince them to buy stock in the Company," or "I must convince them to volunteer to [perform a particular task]." Be as specific as possible. Then, in the right-hand column, indicate **as many WIIFMS as you can think of.** Remember to *think like your partner/customers*—your values probably aren't theirs. What might *they* want? How can this product help fill various holes in *their* hearts?

If a particular WIIFM would matter to only one of the people on your team, indicate that by placing his or her initials next to the WIIFM.

Finally, at the bottom of this page indicate how you would measure success in this particular piece of persuasive communication—what length of time they would work without further raises, for example, or how many people should perform the named task.

PK₁—The <u>Product</u> of my efforts: *List possible WIIFMS:*

_____   _____

_____   _____

_____   _____

_____   _____

_____   _____

_____   _____

                                       _____

                                       _____

                                       _____

                                       _____

                                       _____

How could/would I measure success?

_____

_____

_____

_____

Specific Activity

You can use this page to plan a second project, just as you did the one on the preceding page. The more you do, the better you will become.

PK₁—The <u>Product</u> of my efforts:

List possible WIIFMS:

How could/would I measure success?

CHAPTER 3: COMMUNICATIONS, STEP 1

▲ POWER LISTENING, NEEDS
AND OPEN AND CLOSED PROBES ▲

"That is the essence of science: ask an impertinent question, and you are on the way to a pertinent answer."

—Jacob Bronowski

▲ ## POWER LISTENING, NEEDS
AND OPEN AND CLOSED PROBES ▲

Overview of this Chapter:

If it is true (and it *is* true) that
- the starting point for effective persuasive communication is honoring the fact that normal people are MIBU to themselves,
- that normal people do things that they perceive will satisfy MIBU's need to answer the question "What's In It For Me," and that
- people will agree with us when they believe that what we propose (our "product") will give MIBU enough WIIFMS, then

it follows logically that we need only do three things to become effective persuasive communicators:
- Figure out what our "Product" can do for various MIBUs,
- Figure out what various MIBUs want, and
- Present the appropriate WIIFMs in the right way to each MIBU.

That sounds too easy to be true. And yet the reality is that using the process **is** true, and it **is** that easy.

You started learning how to use it in Chapter 2, where you learned how to analyze the *features* of the change or outcome you desire (your "product") to anticipate possible needs of individual *people.* This introduced you to the three PK's, and all that follows is built on them. This chapter will show you how to *continue* by discovering the needs of the specific person with whom you are working at a given moment in time, by flowing naturally through three roles of **Teacher, Leader** and **Salesperson.** You will do it by adding three more sets of skills and knowledge, which will enable you to match people with preferences in order to achieve the outcome—the "product"—*you* desire. These are knowledge of

- How to plan for a presentation by understanding probable *universal* or "general" human needs;
- How to discover the *unique* needs of a specific MIBU at a particular moment in time, and
- How to *control* a conversation (including directing it to a particular set of conclusions) without being pushy.

These are very powerful skills, Let's take a look at how to possess and use them.

Step One: Understanding general human needs.

While every individual has singular, specific and unique needs, there also are some general needs shared by most people—things like air, food, shelter, and clothing. These shared needs provide a foundation for understanding MIBU's *general* desires, to which we can then add the *specific* needs of a given person at a given time. And since each person is MIBU, she or he is the only one who knows what she or he "needs" at a particular time. That is, *each MIBU is the sole determinant of what he or she "needs." As* the saying goes, in this case, perception most certainly is reality. Let's start this PK_3 process of understanding PK_2 people by considering the needs they are likely to *have in common,* recognizing that even these *common* needs vary over time. For example, someone who is starving does not need the same thing as someone who just finished a large picnic lunch.

What things are people are likely to require at a given moment of time? The easy (some say over-simplified) way of dealing with this is a tool you remember from Psychology 101: Maslow's Hierarchy of needs.

But first, a warning. Before we mention Maslow, let's recognize that in psychology, as in anything human, there are trends and countertrends, based on debates and differences of opinion. One such dialogue exists between the followers of Kurt Lewin, who argued that motivation arises as a result of situational stresses or tensions, and those of Abraham Maslow, who argued that motivation arises as a result of long-term internal needs. For our purposes—as persuaders, rather than therapists—it is less important that we decide who is "right," even if such an answer were possible, than that *we know how to motivate people;* so we shall use **both:** we'll start with Maslow here, and then deal with the issues Lewin raised (in a parallel method) in the next section of this chapter.

As you know, Maslow observed that people have five basic *types* of needs, with the type varying according to the person's immediate circumstances. These were arranged in "levels," with each level having its own specific set of requirements, and thus offering a specific type of motivational opportunity. Each "lower" level had to be satisfied before the next "higher" level could be a motivator. In other words, if you want to motivate someone, you must identify what he or she needs at the level at which they find themselves, and offer that *benefit* to them.

That seems like common sense, and it also has been highly effective for many years. Here are the levels of motivation in Maslow's Hierarchy of Needs:

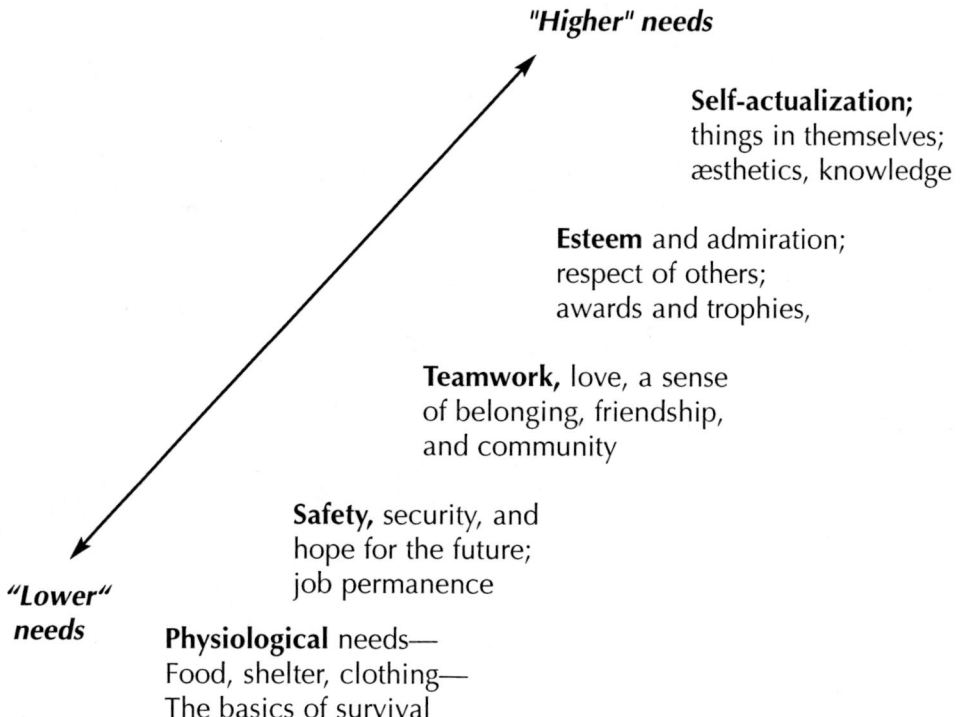

"Higher" needs

Self-actualization;
things in themselves;
æsthetics, knowledge

Esteem and admiration;
respect of others;
awards and trophies,

Teamwork, love, a sense
of belonging, friendship,
and community

Safety, security, and
hope for the future;
job permanence

"Lower"
needs   **Physiological** needs—
Food, shelter, clothing—
The basics of survival

The *means* by which the needs are met varies from society to soci-ety—in the plutocratic Western world, money is the usual means of achieving goals, because it buys things such as food, membership in various groups or communi-ty, insurance, and even the "earning" of recognition. In other cultures, other means—such as social standing, age, or perceived value to the group—serve the same purpose. Yet, obviously, *any* means **loses** power as a motivator as the hier-archy ascends.

Plus, while the items on Maslow's hierarchy are tied to individuals' fiscal or psychic income, always remember that this is *perceived* income: someone who is living on $20,000 a year would be motivated by an amount of money that someone earning $200,000 a year might not notice. The salesperson desperately trying to make quota doesn't care about awards; she or he wants cash; the man-ager with millions in the bank doesn't care about a savings bond; she or he wants esteem and self-actualization. The same rule holds in other cultures, using other means.

You can see where this is taking you. You can get another major PK_2 and PK_3 leg up on things by evaluating the people with whom you work, determining where they are *likely* to be on Maslow's hierarchy. This will prepare you to find WIIFMS more quickly, and more accurately match the right person with the best PK_1 product of your persuasion. You will do this in the Workshops at the end of this Chapter.

Step Two: Understanding a specific MIBU's needs.

As we have seen, Lewin argues that motivation arises as a result of situational stresses or tensions. Again, the goal here is to become a persuasive communicator, rather than a therapist, so the question is not "How did people acquire the particular needs they have at a particular moment," but merely, "How can I discover MIBU's particular needs right now?" For this, we have a truly marvelous tool, built right into your very own head.

A casual examination of the average human being reveals that ears outnumber mouths—the ratio usually is around two-to-one. Many observers have concluded from this design that people should listen twice as much as they talk; yet, every day, others instead follow the example of Samson and kill thousands of opportunities with the jawbone of an ass (see "Judges," Chapter 15, Verses 14-16, in the *Bible*). This provides a great opportunity to anyone who wishes to become a more effective persuasive communicator, because it means that simply *talking less* and *listening more* will give a great advantage. There are some simple techniques that make it easy to do; they are called "power listening" and are the subject of this section of this Chapter.

"Power listening" is asking questions according to a precise method that controls without conflict. It is highly effective for two reasons; the first is *pragmatic,* and the second is *practical.* The practical reason is that unless you know what other people want, you will be unable to provide information to satisfy their WIIFMS. In other words, you must learn from your partner in persuasion before you can provide any information that will matter to him or her.

The pragmatic reason is that listening to another person—and listening carefully, with attention to content—is a great compliment. When you take the time to hear what someone else says, you begin to build a rapport based on perceived mutual appreciation. Thus, your efforts to use your ears twice as much as your mouth will help you on an *emotional* level as well as an *intellectual* one.

With these advantages going for it, you would think that people would be listening to each other all the time. And yet, as we know from personal experience, they aren't. And when they *do* appear to be listening, it's often because they're merely planning what they want to say next. It is very infuriating for people to think *they* are MIBU and want to discuss *themselves* when we feel very strongly they should be talking about *us* (MIBU to ourselves) instead. This same frustration (minus the self-awareness you have acquired by reading this far) occurs in almost everyone you meet and attempt to influence.

This is a great opportunity for someone who wants to communicate effectively and powerfully with others, and makes it obvious that listening skills should be the first of the PK$_3$ processes to make up the repertoire of persuasive communication abilities. And it will be what we are calling *power listening*—that is, doing more than merely allowing sounds to vibrate our eardrums. Instead, we will listen with a game plan, and even control the answers we receive through the kinds of *questions* we ask. This is called the skill of *probing.*

A probe is, of course, an investigative tool; there are many highly specialized probes used in various disciplines. Dentists, for example, have many tiny silvery spikes with which to pry into the nooks and crannies of your teeth and gums; tomb robbers use a long, narrow tube-like instrument called a *spiedo* to find voids in the earth beneath their feet, and spies use all manner of electronic probes to penetrate the worlds of their adversaries. Each of these provides something specific for its user, and each does something that no other tool can accomplish as easily or effectively. When locksmiths use probes to investigate the inner workings of a lock while opening it without a key they use *specific* probes for each specific part of the task. In the same way, you need certain specific probes to gather information, so you can process it for various purposes. Each probe will be used for a precise condition, and works to solve a specific problem.

The three conditions you are likely to encounter when gathering information from another person are
  • Indifference and lack of communication, or
  • Excessive talkativeness and inability to stay "on task," or
  • Clear and useful flow of relevant information.

Two probes can handle all such circumstances; these probes are the heart of power listening. They are called **open** and **closed** probes.

An *open probe* is a question that allows any answer that might occur to the other person. Intentionally non-directional, it allows a flow that can reveal the person's opinion, mind-set, attitudes, method of communication, and much more. A typical open probe used in persuasive communication might be something like one of the following:
  • "What are you hoping to get out of this project?"
  • "How do you feel about our situation right now?"
  • "If you could have any outcome at all, what would it be?"
  • "What matters to you and your family right now?"
  • "What did other solutions to a problem like ours look like?"

Obviously, the answers to these questions could be wide-ranging and very powerful. They might reveal everything in the other person's mind, and the level of detail and way things were said could communicate volumes about his or her priorities—family relationships, personal values and goals, global concerns, and so on.

Sometimes, however, the answers are none of these things—instead, they either are uncommunicative ("Gee, I don't know'" for example), or turn into long, inchoate ramblings. In this case, you need a different probe.

The second type of probe used in power listening is the *closed probe.* This is a question that, unlike the open probe (which intentionally gives the other person no limitations or guidelines on what to say) *actually contains in itself two possible answers, and asks the other person to choose between them.* This "Closed box" makes it much easier for the other person to *provide* information, but makes it much more tedious to *gather* it, since the effective communicator must frame carefully-planned questions that will include reasonable possibilities from which the other person can select an answer.

Here are examples of some good closed probes:
- "Would you prefer a raise or recognition from this project?"
- "Do you think our situation is better or worse than theirs?"
- "Would our situation be improved if we did [example]?"
- "Do you think job security or high income is more important?"
- "Is your family concerned about where you live?
- "Would a perfect world be more like [this] or [that]?"

As you can see, it is very time-consuming to build a complete library of information one page at a time, as happens with closed probes; if you can strike it rich with a single open probe and gather an entire book, you are in luck. But if that *doesn't* happen it's good to have the closed probe as an alternative tool.

But that's not all you can accomplish with a closed probe. This tool can do more. As we noted above there are two primary times when you use closed probes:
- When the other person won't talk (which we just discussed), and
- *When s/he won't shut up.*

The first case is fairly easy to spot and use. If you ask a couple of open probes and get no answer, or no useful answer, you can shift seamlessly to closed probes. The second case is a little harder: if you ask a question and the other person takes off and keeps talking, but without staying on the subject and simply rambles on, you need to take control without seeming to be bulldozing him or her. You can do that by *asking a relevant question about whatever s/he was saying, in the form of a* closed probe.

Please notice two things:

- The closed probe must be a *relevant* question. Luckily, that's easy: simply grab something out of the stream of words coming your way and request clarification or explanation by offering two possible interpretations. That also shows you were listening, which further enhances rapport.
- Second, it must be a *closed* question. If you ask another *open* probe, the other person simply takes off in a new direction and you have accomplished nothing. Describe a box by positing two alternatives, and ask the other person to choose between them. Instantly, you will have the discussion back on target.

There is one last condition that can occur when you are trying to persuade another person, and that is that *you have something **you** want to talk about.* This is very, very important in three circumstances:

- You have identified a solution to the other person's problem and need to introduce it in a positive way, or
- You have an agenda that you want to put on the table, but don't want to seem pushy, or
- There is a specific outcome required for the conversation, and you need to introduce it.

As you know, talking about your own personal MIBU is not nearly as interesting to other people as discussing *theirs.* The closed probe, with its limited answers, will help other people perceive *your* subject as being important to *them.* You simply ask a question (to which you can reasonably expect a "Yes" answer) *pointing at a hidden feature or benefit **to** the other person **of** the product ("goal") you are presenting.*

There is an obvious problem with this tool, of course. It assumes that your guess about what will be important to the other person is accurate. For example, if you assume that your partner wants increased job satisfaction, and you feel that the idea you are proposing would provide that, you run a risk of "shooting blanks"—or, more accurately, firing into a room with no one there—if your partner actually wants shorter hours. Therefore, use closed probes for this purpose only when you are familiar with MIBU's WIIFM needs.

How do you know what questions to ask as closed probes? You simply phrase the possible benefits of your proposed product (as you identified them in the previous step) as questions. Clearly, you cannot do this until you have actually *made* the list of features, and *the longer the list, the better*— since you'll have more probes to use in conversation. You might want to go back to the preceding chapters to improve your Action Step entries before proceeding—don't worry; as Marshall McLuhan pointed out, we'll be waiting for you right here until you get back.

General Activity

Let's go back to the list of people with whom you deal. Make a list of the most important people with whom who work, by name. Then consider the five steps of Maslow's hierarchy and write what they probably find most motivational, right now. Notice that there are several words on the list of Maslow Needs: one person, at the **safety** level, might be motivated by *job security,* while another person at the same level might be more open to concerns about *physical on-the-job safety.* Be alert to such subtleties:

INDIVIDUAL   PROBABLE MASLOW NEED(S)

1. _____   _____

                               _____

2. _____   _____

                               _____

3. _____   _____

                               _____

4. _____   _____

                               _____

5. _____   _____

                               _____

6. _____   _____

                               _____

7. _____   _____

                               _____

8. _____   _____

                               _____

9. _____   _____

                               _____

10. _____   _____

                               _____

Specific Activity

Now do the same for people with whom you are working on your current project:

The project: _____

INDIVIDUAL	PROBABLE MASLOW NEED(S)
1. _____	_____
2. _____	_____
3. _____	_____
4. _____	_____
5. _____	_____
6. _____	_____
7. _____	_____
8. _____	_____
9. _____	_____
10. _____	_____

What are some *closed probes* you can use to verify your assumptions or introduce benefits of your proposed course of action ("product")?

1. _____
2. _____
3. _____
4. _____
5. _____
6. _____

Specific Activity: Comprehensive Action Plan

Prepare for your Effective Professional Persuasive Communication by organizing what you have done so far on this page. (You also can do this on a plain piece of paper, of course.)

The project: _____

The desired outcome: _____

The PK₁ Product Profile for each PK2 Person with whom I am to work:

Person 1: Name _____ Relationship _____

Predictable relationship problems: _____

_____

This person's needs (including Maslow analysis and probing discoveries):

_____

_____

The desired outcome's WIIFMs for this person: _____

_____

_____

Closed probes I could use to inform this person about relevant WIIFMS:
1. _____
2. _____
3. _____

Person 2: Name _____ Relationship _____

Predictable relationship problems: _____

_____

This person's needs (including Maslow analysis and probing discoveries):

_____

_____

The desired outcome's WIIFMs for this person: _____

_____

_____

Closed probes I could use to inform this person about relevant WIIFMS:
1. _____
2. _____
3. _____

Person 3: *Name* _____ *Relationship* _____

Predictable relationship problems: _____

_____

This person's needs (including Maslow analysis and probing discoveries):

_____

_____

The desired outcome's WIIFMs for this person: _____

_____

_____

Closed probes I could use to inform this person about relevant WIIFMS:

1. _____
2. _____
3. _____

Person 4: *Name* _____ *Relationship* _____

Predictable relationship problems: _____

_____

This person's needs (including Maslow analysis and probing discoveries):

_____

_____

The desired outcome's WIIFMs for this person: _____

_____

_____

Closed probes I could use to inform this person about relevant WIIFMS:

1. _____
2. _____
3. _____

Person 5: *Name _____ Relationship _____*
Predictable relationship problems: _____
_____

This person's needs (including Maslow analysis and probing discoveries):
_____
_____

The desired outcome's WIIFMs for this person: _____
_____
_____

Closed probes I could use to inform this person about relevant WIIFMS:
1. _____
2. _____
3. _____

Person 6: *Name _____ Relationship _____*
Predictable relationship problems: _____
_____

This person's needs (including Maslow analysis and probing discoveries):
_____
_____

The desired outcome's WIIFMs for this person: _____
_____
_____

Closed probes I could use to inform this person about relevant WIIFMS:
1. _____
2. _____
3. _____
Continue on a separate piece of paper if necessary, and repeat as often as possible, of course!

CHAPTER 4: PERSUASION, STEP 1

▲ BUILDING RELATIONSHIPS ▲
THROUGH SUPPORT STATEMENTS

"Lord, make us instruments of your peace.
    Where there is hatred, let us sow love;
    Where there is injury, pardon;
    Where there is discord, union;
    Where there is doubt, faith;
    Where there is despair, hope;
    Where there is darkness, light;
    Where there is sadness, joy.
Grant that we may not so much seek
    to be consoled as to console;
    to be understood as to understand;
    to be loved as to love.
For it is in giving that we receive;
it is in pardoning that we are pardoned, and
it is in dying that we are born to eternal life."
                    —A prayer attributed to
                    St. Francis

▲ BUILDING RELATIONSHIPS ▲
THROUGH SUPPORT STATEMENTS

Now you know the basic skills of effective persuasive communication—the foundation upon which to build. You know

- That everyone wants to have what he or she desires, and that there are only three ways of getting that: force, love, or selling.
- That persuasive communication therefore must be viewed as *sales*—conversations that are designed to *make* someone *want* to do something that she or he *needs.*
- That if we wish to be effective at getting our own way, we must learn to think of other people as being as important as we are. Each of us is MIBU, and deserves to be honored and respected.
- That each MIBU is interested in WIIFMs—desirable things that she or he will get out of a situation or circumstance. These WIIFMS can be both *outcome based* (such as getting what s/he wants, which appeals to the rational brain) or *psychologically based* (feeling good about the conversation). Psychologically based outcomes drive the Reptile Brain, which is the seat of intuition.
- That whatever we are trying to achieve in a specific persuasive situation is a *product*—something we are attempting to *sell* to MIBU. Selling requires that MIBU agree to give up something of value in exchange for something she or he desires, and therefore requires work from the Communicator (you).
- That there are some specific tools that help us communicate WIIFMs to MIBU—and one of the first is understanding the three PKs: Product Knowledge (PK_1), People Knowledge (PK_2), and Process Knowledge (PK_3). We are learning Process skills here.
- The first of the PK_3 Process Knowledge steps was learning to think of the PK_1 Product from the perspective of the PK_2 People. This allows us to convert features—descriptive characteristics of the Product— into possible benefits of value to individual MIBUs.
- Then we learned how to discover specific needs of individual MIBUs. There are two sorts of needs: those driven by long-term pressures (as identified by Maslow) and those that are the product of situational stresses (as identified by Lewin). Maslow-type needs are determined by observation, and Lewin-type needs by asking.
- There are two types of questions that work in determining needs: Open probes, that ask broad questions, and Closed probes, that ask MIBU to choose between a pair of option. Closed probes are used with people who talk too little or too much.

Which is all excellent. The question is, "Now what?"

This question is more important than it seems. On the face of it, you'd think that all you have to do is describe the benefits of the product and people would readily agree—after all, it's only logical. But that is where the problem lies: as Mr. Spock, on the TV series *Star Trek®*, was fond of pointing out (or as anyone who has tried to fight the daunting pure logic of a computer knows), human beings are not logical.

If logic were all that you needed, the "New Brain" would sort through the available information and make a reasonable decision. But that is *not* what happens: instead, most decisions are at least a little illogical and some, (especially when the details are too knotty to be readily understood) are *entirely* illogical and the decision is based on trust, faith, or intuition. These three—trust, faith, and intuition— are the *opposite* of knowledge.

Communicating with another person in a way that will appeal to the "Natural Feelings" of his or her Reptile Brain is the most important of the PK_3 skills. It also requires some of the most "Unnatural Acts" you will ever undertake. But if you take the time, you will be able to get what you want, while building relationships with other people based on mutual trust and respect, and even make friends along the way. We're starting that part of the journey now.

Why this matters

As you know, we are all MIBU. Among other things, this means that we want to talk about ourselves, and so does everyone else. It is very annoying to say something only to have the other person reply as if s/he had merely been waiting more-or-less politely for you to shut up so s/he could talk. If, instead, your response to another person's statement both *apparently* and *actually* is a *response* you will truly honor the other person (and show him or her that you are doing it), while advancing the process of acquiring information so you can communicate and persuade. The best form of a response to another person is a specific PK_3 Process tool called a **Support Statement.**

A "Support Statement" is just what its name implies: a *statement* that shows you *support* both the other person and what s/he said. It is a tool, even a trick—but it is a very powerful one. It has three parts, which must be followed *exactly.* Most people automatically use one or two parts of the Statement, but the whole is much greater than its parts. If you can teach yourself to consistently make the statement using all the parts in the format shown, you will be a better communicator and a better-liked person.

Finally, the statement can support not only the other person's **concerns,** but also his or her **values.** This is done by listening to the actual vocabulary used by the other person and incorporating it in the reply. For reasons that you will learn more about later in this book, those words will build bonds based on perceived shared experiences.

The three parts of a Support Statement are as follows:
- Agree with the need expressed by the other person, then
- Introduce a suitable WIIFM feature, and then
- Explain how the feature meets MIBU's needs; why it is a benefit.

Support Statements work because their three parts do three different but related things:
- The first part shows the other person (MIBU) that you are listening, that you understand and accept that person as a human being, that you respect his or her ideas, that you feel their ideas make sense, and that therefore they have a reason to listen to you.
- The second part introduces a piece of relevant information about the proposed product of the conversation, suggesting that it will help the other person achieve something s/he desires—a WIIFM that will come from a single *feature* of the product you recommend.
- The closing step removes any possibility of misunderstanding by actually expanding the feature into a benefit *that the other person has already indicated s/he desires.* And, not only does this make sure that she or he realizes how valuable the feature is, it also thereby reaffirms that you are interested in and concerned about MIBU*. Under the circumstances, no wonder s/he will be interested in listening to your proposal.

It's very important to perform all three steps in order. It's especially important not to lurch straight into the description of your feature, because that would strongly suggest that you're only feigning your interest in MIBU and actually are merely thinking about yourself and your product. Yet this is what most people do when they try to persuade others: and, as we have seen, it does not work.

Again, each of the three steps of the Support Statement, does something very different and important:

- The first step opens MIBU's "window of awareness," by assuring MIBU that the concern she or he raised was valid and important.
- The second provides a fact that will be a WIIFM for MIBU. Instead of being a description of what you are recommending, it instead is a solution to a problem MIBU raised.
- The third expands the feature into a benefit and makes it easy to see what it does for him or her—again reaffirming your support.

More about that on the next page—this is an especially nice PK₃ tool.

In a normal conversation, a Support Statement might sound something like this:

The other person: "I sure would like to be able to get out of here early this Friday. I've got to drive to camp, and it would be a big help to beat rush hour traffic." — *The other person's identified* **need.**

Your three-part Support Statement in reply: "That's a great idea. A few minutes up front would save you a couple of hours at the other end. — *Your statement of* **agreement**

"Look, maybe you could help me get *my* report done right now, and then I could cover for *you* this afternoon, — *Introduce* **feature**

"so you could get out of here early this Friday, drive to camp, and beat rush hour traffic." — *Expand into a* **benefit**—*even repeating MIBU's words.*

Notice that the other person's actual words were repeated back at the end of the Support Statement. That further shows—on a subliminal level—that you were paying attention, because it reveals that you understand the person's *values* as well as his or her *needs.*

Here's a Support Statement in the context of a *probe:*

You: "What's the most important factor in deciding what color to select?" — **Open** *probe*

Customer: "Something new and trendy, I guess." — **Need** *statement*

You: "Great! Yes, you're right, a trendy color can be a great way of jazzing up a space and making it look good for a long time. — *Support Statement Part One:* **Agreement**

"Here, look at this great red. This is the look that's in all the magazines—it's right on the leading edge of the curve. — *Part Two:* **Feature**

"With a color like this, you'll give the space just the look you want—really new and trendy. Cool?" — *Part Three:* **Benefit**

One last time: it is essential to remember that you must use *all three parts* of the Support Statement, *in the correct order,* if you want the tool to work.

• *If you omit the opening statement of agreement*	You do not open the other person's "window of awareness," and they have no reason to listen to you.
• *If you omit the specific feature of your proposal*	You are merely being agreeable. You must add information if you want to persuade someone to act.
• *If you fail to expand the feature into a benefit*	You ask the other person to make the connection between your feature and his or her need. S/He might make it, and might not. Why risk it?

If you use this system and do not repeat the other person's words, it will still work, but not as powerfully. Failing to employ this merely reduces the effectiveness of your reply.

And, if you *fail to use the correct order*—starting with the feature, for example, or ending with the agreement—you don't take advantage of normal human psychology, which *starts* with MIBU and then goes someplace else. Using the format allows the destination to be the place to which you want to take the other person.

This is a mighty and marvelous tool. Use it well, and use it often—it will improve your communications *and* the pleasure people find in being around you. You'll have the chance to practice it in the Action Activities.

"For God's sake don't say yes until I've finished talking."

—Darryl F. Zanuck

Chapter 4
Action Activity

Here are three brief exchanges, in each of which you are told the surrounding circumstances. You have made an open probe, as indicated here, and the other person has replied as shown. *Write a three-part support statement for each example in the space provided.*

The situation: You are trying to convince a friend to go to a Jackie Chan action movie. Your friend claims to be frazzled after a long day.

Your probe: "What would you like to change about how you feel right now?"

The other person's reply: "I'd like to get the office totally out of my head for a while. Quite frankly, the world is too much with me."

Your three-part Support Statement:

(Agree with the need)

_____

_____

_____

(Indicate a suitable feature that will matter to this person)

_____

_____

_____

(Expand the feature into a benefit. Use the other person's words if possible)

_____

_____

_____

Notice that the probe used in this example was <u>open</u>. Now, write a <u>closed</u> probe that would guide the other person even more tightly to the answer you desired—the one you received in this example:

_____

_____

_____

The situation: You are trying to sell your car, a 6 year old Mercedes C-Class, to an acquaintance who has two young children and is concerned about the cost of such a car.

Your probe: "What's the most important thing about a car for your family, especially when you consider your kids?"

The other person's reply: "That's easy—safety. All else is secondary. I want to make sure my kids will be OK if ever I have an accident."

Your three-part Support Statement:

(Agree with the need)

_____

_____

_____

(Indicate a suitable feature that will matter to this person)

_____

_____

_____

(Expand the feature into a benefit. Use the other person's words if possible)

_____

_____

_____

Notice that, again, the probe used in this example was <u>open</u>. Now, write a <u>closed</u> probe that would guide the other person even more tightly to the answer you desired—the one you received in this example. If you really want to be successful, try *two* closed probes:

_____

_____

_____

_____

_____

_____

The situation: You and a coworker are disagreeing about how to make a formal presentation to the Customer. You want to take turns presenting major points, while your coworker wants to have both of you make each point side-by-side.

Your probe: "OK, let me ask you a question. What would be the worst thing that could happen at this presentation."

The other person's reply: "The worst thing? That we look like idiots, and the Customer decides to buy from our competition."

Your three-part Support Statement:

(Agree with the need)

_____

_____

_____

(Indicate a suitable feature that will matter to this person)

_____

_____

_____

(Expand the feature into a benefit. Use the other person's words if possible)

_____

_____

_____

      Notice that, again, the probe used in this example was <u>open</u>. Now, write a <u>closed</u> probe that would guide the other person even more tightly to the answer you desired—the one you received in this example. If you really want to be successful, try *two* closed probes:

_____

_____

_____

_____

_____

_____

Specific Activity

Return to the Comprehensive Specific Activity in the previous chapter. Please take those six of those WIIFMS (especially good ones, of course) and, here and on the following page, copy
- One of the WIIFMS and the
- CLOSED probes that would call attention to each of them.
- ***Then write a three-part Support Statement for that WIIFM,*** assuming you got a "yes" reply to your probe.

FIRST WIIFM: _____

CLOSED PROBE: _____

_____

THREE-PART SUPPORT STATEMENT:
Agree: _____

Feature: _____

Benefit: _____

_____

SECOND WIIFM: _____

CLOSED PROBE: _____

_____

THREE-PART SUPPORT STATEMENT:
Agree: _____

Feature: _____

Benefit: _____

_____

THIRD WIIFM: _____

CLOSED PROBE: _____

_____

THREE-PART SUPPORT STATEMENT:
Agree: _____

Feature: _____

Benefit: _____

_____

FOURTH WIIFM: _____

CLOSED PROBE: _____

_____

THREE-PART SUPPORT STATEMENT:
Agree: _____

Feature: _____

Benefit: _____

_____

FIFTH WIIFM: _____

CLOSED PROBE: _____

_____

THREE-PART SUPPORT STATEMENT:
Agree: _____

Feature: _____

Benefit: _____

_____

SIXTH WIIFM: _____

CLOSED PROBE: _____

_____

THREE-PART SUPPORT STATEMENT:
Agree: _____

Feature: _____

Benefit: _____

_____

The more time you spend on this activity, the better you will do as an effective persuasive communicator. There is no substitute for practice when learning a skill, as we saw above; please think of this as hitting your 1000 golf balls, focussing on your salads, or riding those six hours a day on your bicycle. It will reward you.

"Practice doesn't make perfect. Only perfect practice makes perfect."

—Vince Lombardi

CHAPTER 5: PROJECTION:

▲   TWO TOOLS IN ONE   ▲

"Whatever your heart clings to and relies upon, that is really your God. (Woruf du nun . . . dein Herz hängt und verlässt, das ist eigentlich dein Gott.)."

—Martin Luther
The Large Catechism

▲ ## Two Tools in One ▲

Projection—seeing or admiring one person's interests in, or projecting them on another—is a common human tendency. It has two forms, both of which are very valuable for the Effective Persuasive Communicator; specifically, you can use it to:

- Discover the attitudes and values of other people, so you can analyze their personalities;
- Select appropriate features to convert into benefits when making a presentation;
- Prepare yourself to handle possible objections by understanding real concerns.

Let's first look at the simpler form—heroes and hero-worship. To begin this study, let's start with yourself. Please list below four people you admire. They can be people from any walk of life: personal friends or family, historical figures, contemporary or past athletes, entertainers, artists or political figures; they can be heroes or villains in the eyes of the world—indeed, any people at all, as long as they have earned your admiration. Then, for each person you have listed, please select five words or short phrases that describe him or her.

WORKSHOP: LOOKING INWARD

I admire these people: | **Five words or phrases that describe each of these persons:**

A. _____ 1._____ 2._____

3._____ 4._____ 5._____

B. _____ 1._____ 2._____

3._____ 4._____ 5._____

C. _____ 1._____ 2._____

3._____ 4._____ 5._____

D. _____ 1._____ 2._____

3._____ 4._____ 5._____

Application 1: Projecting other people on ourselves

There are many ways we reveal ourselves, often without realizing what we're doing. One of these—and one that is especially useful to the Effective Persuasive Communicator—is the way people choose heroes to admire and revere. These heroes are people whose values and perceived virtues we acquire vicariously by projecting them on ourselves, through appropriation, just as someone wearing an athletic jersey with a real player's name or number "takes on" that person's identity.

The concept of heroes (and the related concept of hero-worship) is not fashionable at the present time in the politically-correct United States. The idea that one person might be more exceptional, or contribute more to the common good, than another, is offensive to the PC crowd, just as it was to the Soviets who preceded them: an old Russian maxim is, "The nail that stands up highest is the one that gets hit down hardest."

It is easier to argue the opposite—that the presence or absence of heroes can be observed in the actions of others. For example, the Tampa Bay Buccaneers before and after the arrival of one man—head coach, Jon Gruden—were two very different football teams. The works of William Shakespeare were produced not by a committee or a force of history, but by one man. Rosa Parks set off an entire movement when, as she put it, "My only concern was to get home after a hard day's work," and she refused to relinquish her seat to move to the back of the bus. These people were individuals who changed things, and each is a hero to many.

Of course, for most normal human beings these sophisticated (or counterproductive) arguments are unimportant, if they even are aware of them. Rather, they tend automatically to identify—and identify *with*—the "heroes" of life, in what both Thomas Carlyle and Will Durant called "hero worship." The reasons for hero-worship (while interesting to speculate about) are not relevant here; what is *useful* is the fact that *the person selected as a personal "hero" by another person has certain abilities, characteristics and traits. Those characteristics are at some level important to the person who selects that particular "hero" and that fact reveals a great deal about the other person.*

A simple example is the late stock car driver, Dale Earnhardt. His untimely accidental death sanctified him in the minds of many fans. Yet when he was alive he was famous for a particular kind of sly roughness on the track that caused more than one accident over the years—"I just gave him a little tap," he would say when someone would complain that Earnhardt had purposely run into his car. "That's how it is in stock car racing." (He was giving just such a "little tap" when he lost control of his car and rammed into a wall at high speed on the last race of his life.)

People who considered him a hero while he was alive sported Dale Earnhardt's "Number 3" on their cars and pickup trucks. And long ago, plant managers in various companies noticed that an associate who identified with Dale Earnhardt's number also shared many aspects of his personality. Often, these people were very independent, and they enjoyed competition; in some cases they could be antisocial and infrequently even display passive-aggressive tendencies. They liked to work and play hard, and admired such strength in others—as they did in their hero, whom they called "Iron Head" and "The Intimidator," the man who loved "swapping paint and banging bumpers." In short, they had found a way of articulating their own values.

This is what usually happens when anyone identifies with a hero. Certain characteristics make the hero attractive and they fuse into one in the hero-worshiper's eyes. Then, the admirers project the **heroes'** values on **themselves,** and might even manifest exterior characteristics of the hero (dress, walk, hairstyle) by conscious or unconscious imitation. Once those **characteristics** are understood, the **real person** with whom you work (and his or her **values**) can be understood as well.

*However, it is extremely important not to confuse **your** values with those of **other** people. That is why you listed **characteristics** for the people you admire in this chapter—you may admire someone for reasons other people don't perceive.* A couple of examples:

•Once, when studying this chapter, a woman came up to say she was perplexed. Her husband, she said, was a gentle and loving man who showed no aggressive characteristics at all, and yet he had been such a dedicated admirer of Dale Earnhardt that they had attended many races just to watch him drive. When asked what her husband had admired, she replied that it was his *dedication, professionalism, hard work* and *overcoming the obstacle of having had a childhood with limited opportunities.* Then she realized that the Dale Earnhardt who was her husband's hero was not the glaring, terrifying nemesis of the race track—it was the man she admired her husband for being.

•Another woman noted that she had selected Princess Diana of Wales and Mother Theresa of Calcutta as heroes, and that those seemed to be opposite people—one, the heir of a privileged life who died violently while pursuing pleasure, and the other, a saintly woman who in the same week died in the Order she had built to tend to others. Again, once this woman looked at her *words,* she had praised both her heroes for the same things: she perceived they were equally selfless, concerned for others, loving, focused on showing God's mercy to wounded people. The dichotomy—if there is one—is in the world's **perception** of this woman's heroes, not her own values.

71

Also, please note that this analytical method usually does not apply to groups, such as sport teams. Association with a sports team usually is based on such accidents as geography or history. If, however, a group is clearly identified with a set of values or its own leader—the U.S. Naval Academy or Dallas Cowboys football teams in the days of Roger Staubach, for example—there are useful implications.

It is very easy to discover another person's heroes. Usually, the information comes out in the course of normal chitchat; if not, asking a direct question can bring it out. And once you have identified another person's hero, you can analyze the underlying values and interests, gaining greater understanding of your partner. There are many ways you can discover what those values are, but the simplest and best is to *simply ask the other person what she or he admires about his or her hero.* The things admired by the other person allow you to:

- ***Understand him or her,*** using tools you will learn in Chapters 7 and 12.
- ***Select appropriate features*** to convert into benefits relevant to his or her needs, using skills you learned in Chapter 2 and 4 of this little book.

Let's test this system. A few pages ago you listed 20 words that described *people* you admire. Please copy those words here:

_____ _____

_____ _____

_____ _____

_____ _____

_____ _____

_____ _____

_____ _____

_____ _____

_____ _____

_____ _____

Reflect on this list. These are *things* you admire. By performing this exercise with other people, you can learn the same about them, so you can honor them as the MIBUs they are.

For many people, the exercise on the previous page is discomfiting. Some people actually get defensive or even angry about what they have found. If that is the case with you, fine; you may be lying to yourself, either when you select your list of heroes, or when you deny what you have found. ***But whether you are being honest or not, other people will do more good than ill by manifesting the values you admire.*** In this way, they can show that they realize you are MIBU.

If you still disagree, please disregard this chapter and go on to the next. No harm is done, and no insult is intended. However, the Present Author is reminded of the story of the man who went to a psychologist for analysis.

The psychologist decided to conduct a Rorschach test. Upon seeing the first ink blot, the patient said, "That's easy. That's a naked woman." The psychologist then showed another ink blot, and the patient quickly observed, "Obvious. That's two naked women and a naked man." In response to the third ink blot, the patient said, "Hmm—three naked women, a hat, and a tractor." The psychologist continued, and the patient made the same sort of discovery in each test image.

Finally, the psychologist said, "You know, it's a little inappropriate for me to make this observation, but you certainly seem obsessed with naked people." The patient sat up straight, looked at the psychologist, and said, "Me? ***You're*** the one with all the dirty pictures!"

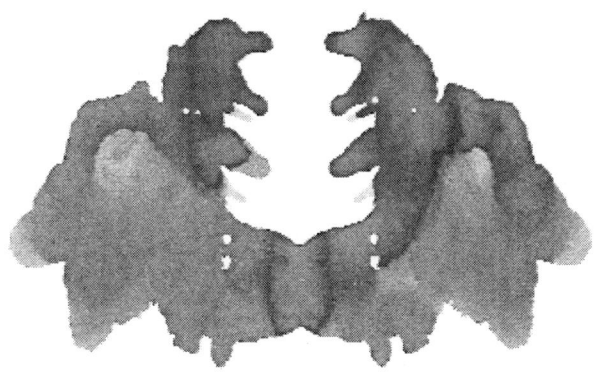

Application 2: Projecting ourselves on other people

The second way projection can help you seems a little odder at first, but will be of immense value in helping you anticipate objections, prevent them, and/or handle them successfully should this occur. It is based on the fact that most people do not tell the whole truth when things are not going the way they want.

Specifically, when someone disagrees with another person, she or he is unlikely to speak openly about the source of the disagreement. This is because the source of the disagreement causes pain, and sensible people like to avoid pain as much as possible. Therefore, if there is something that upsets someone, the thing they are least likely to discuss is the actual reason for their discomfort.

But if someone else is upset, and we don't know why, we are unable to correct the problem. What, then, are we to do? The answer, again, is the word **projection,** but in an interestingly different way.

In this form of projection, we ask another person's opinion, but not by asking directly what she or he thinks. Instead, we ask that person to describe **how an imaginary third person would feel about the situation—** not how **he** or **she** feels, but **how the imaginary other person feels.** Then, he or she will reveal his or her beliefs by projecting them onto the other person.

For example, if we ask someone to go see a particular movie with us, and she/he replies that she/he doesn't feel like it, we have no way of responding persuasively. If we repeat the question, the other person will feel almost compelled to repeat the vague objection—probably in an annoyed tone—and we will not only not advance the conversation, but also may even inflict slight harm on the relationship.

On the other hand, if we say instead, "I understand! There's a lot of things we could do this weekend so we both could have real recreation. Let me ask you: What have people been saying about that movie?" we are likely to get the person's true feelings, **projected onto the imaginary "people."** Then the issues can be addressed, **or** another movie chosen. [Please notice the use of the **Three Part Support Statement** in this example—see Chapter 4 for a refresher, if you wish.]

This tool is very powerful, and—although you may have to use it a couple of times to get the true responses—ultimately very reliable.

There are two **caveats** to remember.

The first is, **don't ask the other person to project his or her feelings onto a real person.** In this case, a thoughtful person might reveal a penetrating understanding of a specific third party's value systems—which will be useless in handling **his** or **her** feelings.

The second is, **don't allow the other person to become defensive about his or her opinion.** This is completely counterproductive. You can prevent this by the simple tool of making a **focused support statement.**

(You remember this skill from Chapter 4. It consists of three steps:

- **Agree with an underlying need expressed by the other person.** Make certain that you don't paint yourself into a corner; if they make a vague and indeciferable statement like, "I just don't think that we can work together on this project," **don't** agree by saying "Yes, you really are an insufferable jerk, and so am I!" Instead, agree with something like "I understand. It's vital that you have a supportive relationship with your suppliers."

- **Make a relevant positive statement that redefines the conversation.** In the above example, you might say, "And the most important thing is that they understand your real needs and concerns, so they can act as allies." In this way, you both **support your product without disagreeing with the other person,** while at the same time you **change the conversation from "working together" to "being an ally."**

- Then, make a **very slight benefit statement** and then shift into your projection question. In this case, it might be, "I know you are as committed to that as I am. What do you think **the other people on your team** are looking for in **their** vendors on this project?")

Like most of the skills of Effective Persuasive Communication, this seems harder than it is, but it becomes easier with practice. The practice must take two forms: **making support statements** and **using projection techniques.** At this point in the book, we assume that you know the former already; to be on the safe side, we're going to test that in the Action Activities. If you find this challenging, please review the earlier chapters.

Then we'll go practice the projection step.

General Activity

As usual, we need to take the information on **using projection to understand other's values** in this chapter from the essential introductory but merely theoretical world of information acquisition, into the hardscrabble world of applied **information application.** This means that we need to practice the new skills in a way that will have real-world applications.

Obviously, we are constrained by your present memories of people who are important to you. If you don't have any suitable knowledge, please skip the first question for now and go to Questions 2 and 3, but please complete Question 1 at some time, for your own sake.

1. Identify a target for study—someone important to your life or work:

_____

Identify someone that she/he admires—sports figure, entertainer, political figure, historical character, personal friend, anything:

_____

List five or more words that she/he uses to describe this person:

_____   _____   _____   _____

_____   _____   _____   _____

What does this tell you about your target contact?

   Obviously, you want to continue this exercise as much as possible.

2. Phrase a question that you would feel comfortable using to discover someone else's hero(es):

_____

_____

_____

3. Here are some objections that someone might raise in a persuasive conversation. Please think of good projection questions you could ask to determine what she or he is really thinking.

"This product really isn't something I would specify."
Your projecting question:

_____

_____

"I don't want to see an *opera*, for goodness' sake."
Your projecting question:

_____

_____

"I'm very happy with my current vendors and don't need any more."
Your projecting question:

_____

_____

"We really shouldn't be doing this you know."
Your projecting question:

_____

_____

"This is not an attractive option."
Your projecting question:

_____

_____

"There's something I don't like here, but I can't put my finger on it."
Your projecting question:

_____

_____

Specific Activity

Reflect over the project you are using for this practice. First, you will want to discover the hero(es) of the MIBUs with whom you are working; this will require you to have some suitable questions about important people in their interests or histories. You also will need to be able to dig below the surface, in order to identify the *things they admire* about those heroes, *and you must do it in a way that is congenial both for the person **you** are **and** for each other person.* Here, think up and write down suitable questions to identify their heroes:

Your question to identify [insert name:_____]'s heroes:

_____

_____

Your question to identify [insert name:_____]'s heroes:

_____

_____

Your question to identify [insert name:_____]'s heroes:

_____

_____

Your question to identify what they admire in their heroes:_____

_____

_____

_____

_____

Now, imagine objections that might be raised to your proposal. What are some effective questions you could ask that would give you insight into the true nature of those objections, by allowing the other person to project his or her feelings onto imaginary "other people"?

A good "projecting" question:_____

_____

_____

Another question:_____

_____

CHAPTER 6: COMMUNICATIONS, STEP 2

▲ INFORMATION ACQUISITION ▲

"Speech was given to humans so they could disguise their thoughts." ("La parole a été donnée à l'homme pour deguiser sa pensée.")
—Charles-Maurice de Talleyrand

Any quick examination of a group of people reveals an almost baffling variety of appearances and attitudes. While the basic equipment is fairly constant within two broad categories (distinguished by sexual characteristics), the individual variations are stunning: skin colors range from white to black, with hues of red, yellow, and brown in between; hair can be any of several colors (including some not included in the genetic code), absent, or arranged in an almost infinite variety of shapes; voices normally cover a range of 1½ octaves (and in extremes range across 3 more), and so on. With such amazing diversity in the ways we are equipped and presented to the world, it should come as no surprise to learn that there are great variations in the way things operate *inside* our heads and bodies as well. Understanding and responding with dignity and respect to those variations are a major tool of the effective persuasive communicator, and the subject of over half of this book.

One such variation is in the way individual human beings acquire information. MIBU automatically assumes that his or her way is the norm for all people, of course, and often is surprised to learn that the opposite is true. In fact, the odds are overwhelming that at any given moment each person on the planet—including the reader of this sentence—is *out of communications synchronization with the vast majority of the people in his or her life.*

This is because there are many elements and tools of communication, and each has its own systems and rules. The first one that we shall consider here is how people *acquire information.*

There are three primary learning channels, and each person has a personal favorite (and assumes every other MIBU has the same one). The three possible ways of acquiring information are by
- Seeing,
- Hearing, or
- Experiencing.

This is not to imply that the individual person's learning channel is exclusive (that is, each person uses only one channel, or only one channel at a time). Nor is it to imply that a given person's channel might not change, even in the midst of a conversation—in fact the opposite is true. Channels *do* shift, and often they shift *rapidly;* therefore, the ability to read another person's communications channel at any given moment is a major persuasive advantage. Learning this skill, and knowing how to apply it swiftly and consistently, gives someone a huge persuasive advantage. And, luckily, this is an especially easy PK_3 skill to master.

However, while it is easy to master, at the same time it is complicated by the fact that there are *two* ways of accomplishing the *same* end. Therefore, we'll break this skill into two parts, dealing with it first here, and then later—in chapter 10—again in greater detail.

To begin, please compare the following short paragraphs, identical in content:

"Let's talk about one of the best-sounding skills of the persuasive communicator—something that lets you tell people how to speak and listen in a totally new way. Once you hear this, you can relate stories about other people's lessons that your partners will hear and understand that your words can help them to a day of harmony."

"Let's examine one of the best-looking skills of the persuasive communicator—something that shows how you can get people to see things in a totally new way. Once you get the picture, you can sketch out an image that will show them a vision of the future that will make them see you as someone who can show them to a brighter day."

"Let's get our hands on one of the most powerful skills of the persuasive communicator—something that lets you help people to share in a totally new experience. Once you own this, you can give other people skills that will open up an exciting future, to make them understand that you can help them to a day of pride and satisfaction."

If you reflect on these three, you'll quickly see that each makes the same promise: to give you the opportunity to help others, in such a way that they will appreciate you and your advice. And you'll also feel as if one of the three is somehow *better* than the other two—it just makes more *sense*.

Now reflect back on the details of the three paragraphs, and you'll notice that the first uses words of *sound* almost exclusively—the words of story-telling, narratives, and conversation. The second paragraph communicates the same ideas, but uses words taken from *sight*—words like "see" and "show" instead of "hear" and "tell." The third paragraph goes in another direction still: it uses words of *feeling and emotion*. While the first paragraph offers a *harmonious* day, the second a *brighter* one, and the third a day of *pride and satisfaction*.

Needless to say, by discovering which of the paragraphs you prefer intuitively, you have gained an insight into your *own* communications style—the one you preferred is probably the one most like you (since you are MIBU, after all).

What happens in the real world is that each of us acquires information in the method we find most congenial and comfortable. If our primary style is visual, we tend to learn by reading books, magazines, and articles; when in doubt, we tend to look for written proof.

If our primary style is auditory, we tend to learn by hearing things; we like the telephone and even can enjoy meetings. We rarely take notes, but remember most of what we're told. When in doubt, we tend to seek out testimonials, or we ask for narratives to allay our fears.

If our primary style is experiential, we tend to learn by doing things; we like moving bits of cloth or paper around, and we rarely read instruction manuals. When in doubt, we tend to trust what we can prove through our own experiences. Often, we're very touchy-feely.

This, then, is the language *of languages*—the way our words reveal the way we *acquire information.* This is very important, for two reasons: first, because we *screen out* or even block knowledge that doesn't pass through our personal style filters, and second because we *respond more warmly* to people who are like us.

What are we to do with this knowledge? Three things.

First, it is very important to recognize that, if there are three communications styles and we have one of them, in all probability we are **out of synchronization with two out of three people** we meet. This means you must *expect* failure in communication unless you adapt to it. [In fact, the differences are not evenly distributed among the populations: almost 50% are primarily visual, 30% auditory, and 20% experiential. Incomes are distributed unevenly, too; most of the highly-paid professions (lawyers, physicians, executives) attract readers, and the lower-paid professions attract doers. This is far from exact, however; there are many wealthy plumbers and many impoverished teachers.)

Second, we need to build in necessary accommodations for other people, recognizing that they have as much a right to be MIBU as we do. If you are a vision-type person, who gets information through your eyes, you need to respect and honor those people who don't read your reports, and instead want to *ask questions* or *do things with your evidence.* If you are a hearing-type person, whose primary sense of perception is the ear, you need to accept the people who don't want to talk on the phone, or who seem impatient when you share your stories. And if you are a feeling-type person, you must understand those people who seem unexcited, or don't get involved in your desire to experiment, play with things, get emotional, or try new stuff.

Third, we must build in adaptations of our presentation styles. If you are visual, for example, you must recognize that *about 50% of the people with whom you deal will be unmoved by your pictures, charts, and graphs.* You are Ross Perot in front of Larry King, and unless you sit down and start talking you are dead in the water.

Similarly, *everyone* needs to decide how to present the *same* information to *all three* types of people, if they want to be effective persuaders. This can take some effort, sometimes, but it's often easier than it seems at first.

For example, if a *visual* person were to argue the superiority of a particular *color* to an auditory person, s/he would be prepared with *stories and testimonials* about the success other people had with it; if presenting the color to an *experiential* person, s/he would have samples of various colors and materials with which the other person could play to build *ownership of and confidence* in the choice. The *visual* speaker would *not* simply hold up colors and expect other people to "see" them as well as s/he did.

Of course, you may be wondering if it is possible to shift methods, or have combinations of methods at the same time. Absolutely; this is treated in detail in Chapter 10. For now, let's remember KISS—**K**eep **I**t **S**ublimely **S**imple—and think in terms of the three main information acquisition styles alone. There's plenty of time for more detail (and consequent confusion) later.

If you have received this book as part of a seminar, you will now have discovered something else: all three methods of communication are employed in this presentation. The ideas are *read* in this book, *discussed* in the live presentations, and *worked out* in the Action Activities. And the book itself, you will notice, consciously uses words from all three methods, although the present author's personal preference for the written word is never far from the fore. (If you got this book without attending a seminar, and have gotten this far, you almost certainly are a reader, or possibly an experiential; the hearers never got to this point.)

Finally, please remember that we have only *begun* this conversation in this chapter. For more detail, please stay tuned and wait for chapter 10; for now, please turn to the Action Activities—especially all you experientials.

Chapter 6
Action Activity

Let's return to Chapter 1's Action Activity, where you made a list of the people with whom you habitually work. You will need to observe them very carefully, to determine their preferred methods of acquiring information. The easiest and most reliable way is listening to the words they use in everyday conversation (other than conversations in which one of the channels is the *subject*, obviously), and counting how many come from each of the three "families" of words—auditory, experiential, or visual. The result, expressed as a percentage, is that person's probable information acquisition style *at this time*. (Another method of acquiring this information is presented later in this book.)

Each person, by name:	*His/her primary communication channel*	*Secondary communication channel, if any.*
_____	_____	_____
_____	_____	_____
_____	_____	_____
_____	_____	_____
_____	_____	_____
_____	_____	_____
_____	_____	_____
_____	_____	_____
_____	_____	_____
_____	_____	_____
_____	_____	_____
_____	_____	_____
_____	_____	_____

Specific Activity

Do the same thing with the people in the current or upcoming project identified in Chapter 1:

The project: _____

Each person, by name:	His/her primary communication channel	Secondary communication channel, if any.
_____	_____	_____
_____	_____	_____
_____	_____	_____
_____	_____	_____
_____	_____	_____
_____	_____	_____
_____	_____	_____
_____	_____	_____

In general, what are some critical aspects of this project that would be intrinsically attractive to each of the three communication channel types? That is, what are the obvious "hot buttons" for this project? **Notice: you should be able to come up with roughly the same** *number* **of hot buttons for each type; if it's hard, keep at it until you do.**

Hot buttons for VISUALS:	for AUDITORIES:	for EXPERIENTIALS:
_____	_____	_____
_____	_____	_____
_____	_____	_____
_____	_____	_____
_____	_____	_____

CHAPTER 7: COMMUNICATIONS, STEP 3:

▲   LINEAR VERSUS ASSOCIATIVE,   ▲
CASUISTIC VERSUS HOLISTIC,
AND
VERSUS

"The main difference between men and women is that men are lunatics and women are idiots"

—Rebecca West

Recent years have shown some very interesting research results in the ways people process information—what the "world views" beneath their day-to-day thinking are, in other words. Some of this has been fairly trivial, best suited for the sensational journals, while other has been very scholarly and potentially quite useful. When you are dealing with other people, trying to find ways to become a more effective persuasive communicator, these could be very valuable and helpful.

Before we begin, however, we must acknowledge the benefits of generalized observation while ignoring and moving beyond the dangerous limitations of stereotyping. The difference is that *generalized knowledge*, based on research and observation, provides a *starting point* for individual human understanding, while a stereotype constitutes an *ending.*

For example, if you saw several men each of whom was over 7'8" tall walking together, and if you knew that a basketball team were in the neighborhood, you would be justified in hypothesizing that they were the team of which you had heard, and testing the hypothesis by asking them. That would be using your generalized knowledge as a starting point for communication, saving time by avoiding other, wasteful possibilities (Might those men be jockeys? Gymnasts? An accidental agglomeration? Possible, but less likely.)

On the other hand, if you knew that I was Dutch, and if you had heard that all people from the Netherlands were hard-headed and impossibly blunt in their speech, and if as a consequence of that you avoided me and told other people I was hard to get along with, you would be indulging in a stereotype. You were not using knowledge, but rather accretized opinion; you would be assuming, not testing; and ending, not beginning, the learning process.

In the same way, the subject of this chapter, while potentially powerful, must be understood as the *summary of research that can start your study of individuals,* rather than hard-and-fast rules that you should accept at face value. This is especially true because the research deals with two potentially explosive categories: men and women, and Asian and European value systems and patterns of thought. The present writer prefers the terms *linear* and *associative,* and *holistic* and *casuistic,* respectively, but must acknowledge the terms in common use.

Linear versus Associative;
Men versus Women

In 1992, John Gray published a book titled *Men are from Mars; Women are from Venus,* and soon became very wealthy. He demonstrated some very simple and predictable differences between the way men and women think, and argued that understanding these differences would improve relations between the sexes (which, obviously, is not the same as sexual relations, although there may be consequential elements).

In all seriousness, many people found that using his techniques greatly improved interpersonal communication. The problem is that (as Gray himself noted) many men "think like women" (to use the popular understanding of the terms), and many women "think like men."

This has no bearing on their sexual identity or attitude; it simply means that there are two ways of thinking *which tend to be concentrated in gender differences, but which can be used by anybody.* In fact, the best thinkers *combine the two methods*, since each brings something different to the table.

The present writer, therefore prefers to avoid the sensational title that made Gray wealthy (which may not be a smart move on the present writer's part), and instead offers two ideas to improve your effectiveness as a persuasive communicator:

- First, there are two ways of thinking, which can be found in people of both sexes. These ways may be called *linear* (that is, tending to go more-or-less in a straight line from a question to an answer) and *associative* (that is, tending to explore alternatives around a question and consider various related ideas while deciding on an answer). In Gray's terms, "men" tend to be "linear," and "women" tend to be "associative," but—again—the present author warns against excessive generalizations.
- Second, it is very rare for someone to be *entirely* linear or associative; the "yin" and "yang" of male/female duality is never more real than when it comes to the way the mind works. Therefore, the reader is advised to think in terms of people's ways of thinking as *lying on points of a continuum,* rather than being stuck at an extreme.

"NEUTRAL"

LINEAR		ASSOCIATIVE
THINKING		THINKING

Holistic versus Casuistic;
Asian versus European

Another, equally interesting study was released in 2000 by The University of California. There, researchers decided to try to quantify the often-observed differences between Asian and European families' world-views. They used as subjects students of Asian extraction, whose families lived in the United States, attending various campuses of the University, as compared to students of typically European background.

Psychological testing revealed very significant differences in values and attitudes, all the more remarkable for the fact that the participants were *naturalized* residents of the United States; from this fact, the researchers extrapolated that the differences would be even greater if native Asians were compared to native Europeans.

What were the differences? Simply stated, Asian students tend to view the world from the standpoint of the *family unit*, while European-based students tend to view the world from the standpoint of *individuals*. Even more important, the Asian students tended to see the world, and the things that happen to people, to be interconnected, giving them a **holistic** view of life, while the European students tended to see the individual as determining his or her own fate (and ultimately being responsible for his or her own happiness), leading to a world view that could be called **casuistic**.

A logical expansion of this idea is that Asian students tended to believe that if one works for the greater good of the group, the individual will be taken care of as well, while the European students tended to believe the opposite: if the individuals take care of themselves, the group will be OK, too. The obvious implications for attitudes toward elders and children, relationship to the State, and other global differences are important, but will not be addressed here.

There are many interesting consequences of these differences of opinion, which are discussed below. However, it is also very important to recognize that few people exist at the extremes described above; as with linear/associative differences, most people lie somewhere on a *continuum* of belief, between the two poles.

	"NEUTRAL"	
HOLISTIC		CASUISTIC
THINKING		THINKING

(Comparable research has not yet been done on other national groups, which is OK—since we are intentionally considering these as <u>attitudes</u>, rather than racial stereotypes.)

Linear/Associative; Holistic/Casuistic Combined

Once we grow beyond the ultimate incest—a love-affair with ourselves—we can understand, respond, honor, and respect the needs of other people, and in the process become effective persuasive communicators. This is vitally important in the area of understanding how other people *process information*; how they see the world (or "hear" or "experience" it, for audials and experientials). Combining what we have just learned produces a neat four-quadrant model called a Cartesian Coordinates grid, on which the first parameter of the model places other people on the *Associative to Linear* continuum, and the second on the *Holistic to Casuistic* one (with very few people at the extremes of either line). The terms used by other researchers are included in the quadrants for reference.

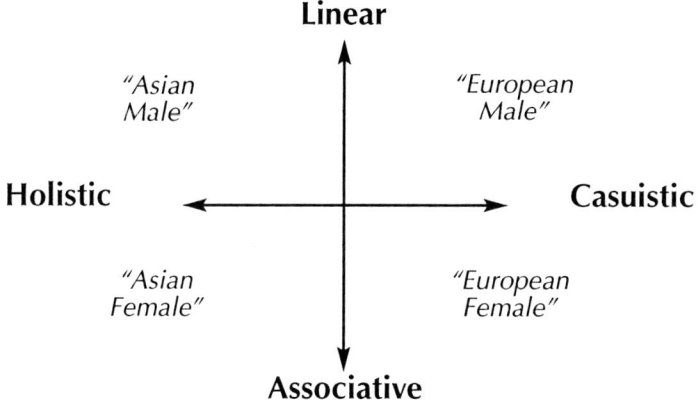

The Present Author prefers the following labels, showing the sorts of personalities one is likely to encounter with theses world-views:

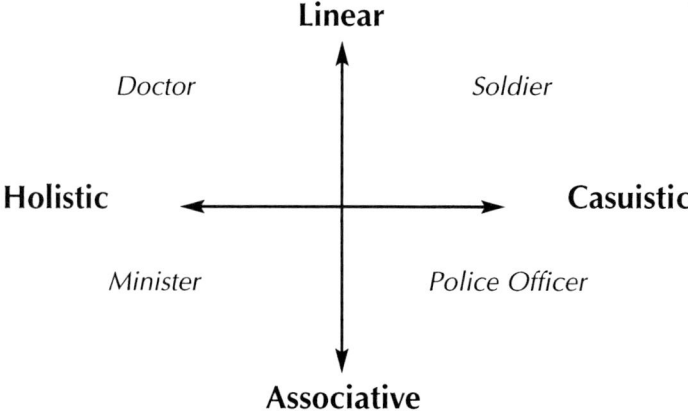

Remember, the goal of this tool (like all the tools in this book) is neither *pigeonholing* nor *stereotyping* people. It is *understanding them* so you can *demonstrate respect and a shared purpose*—"community," in a word. All you need do is learn how to **identify** the four *characteristics;* then you can decide how to **respond** to the four processing *styles.*

And remember again that it is very unlikely that you will encounter people who are at the extremes of either "arm" of the coordinates. Most people are mixtures of beliefs and attitudes, so they will fall *somewhere along each of the two lines,* rather than at the ends. You merely decide on *which side of* center they fall on the two arms, determining whether they are more *linear* or more *associative* when they approach a *task,* and more *holistic* or *casuistic* when they think about individual *outcomes.* That will tell you their *information-processing style.*

Here are some markers that define the ends of the **task** arm:

LINEAR PEOPLE

Preferences
Staying "on task"
Keeping the group small
Step-by-step thinking
Remembering the desired goal
Speaking directly and plainly
One-on-one relationships

Say things like
"I want..."
"Stay on the point."
"My opinion is..."
"Let's make a quick decision."
"We can handle this."

Act
Brusque
Decisive
Impatient
Methodical
Particular

ASSOCIATIVE PEOPLE

Preferences
Considering alternatives
Making the group inclusive
Brainstorming
Making the process work
Being oblique and sensitive
Meetings

Say things like
"The group needs ..."
"Consider these ideas."
"Do you think ..."
"Let's take our time."
"Let's get others involved."

Act
Indirect
Contemplative
Attentive
Scatter-brained
Accommodating

*Before continuing—consider yourself. Where on the line do you think **you** fall? What is **your** preferred or natural attitude to processing information?*

	"NEUTRAL"	
LINEAR		ASSOCIATIVE
THINKING		THINKING

Here are some markers that define the ends of the *outcomes* arm:

HOLISTIC PEOPLE

Preferences
Think in terms of family
Value tradition
Aware of rules and decorum
Usually political liberal
Respect authority

Say things like
"What are the implications?"
"It's our responsibility."
"Let's get consensus."
"What will this do?"
"Is this the right thing to do?"

Act
Friendly, open
Gentle motions and voice
In (question themselves)
Environmentally sensitive
Like Mr. Rogers

CASUISTIC PEOPLE

Preferences
Think in terms of individual
Admire strength
Likely to be independent
Usually political conservative
Dislike authority

Say things like
"Can I trust this?"
"It's his own fault."
"Let's get accountability."
"What will this cost?"
"Does this work?"

Act
Closed, distant
Choppy motions and speech
Out (question others)
More aware of other issues
Like Mr. T

*Again, consider yourself. Where on this line do you think **you** fall? How does this shape **your** preferred or natural way of processing information?*

```
                        "NEUTRAL"
HOLISTIC                    |                        CASUISTIC
THINKING                    |                         THINKING
```

Now, place yourself on the Cartesian Coordinate grid by drawing lines from your self-assessment on the arms and identifying the quadrant in which you fall.

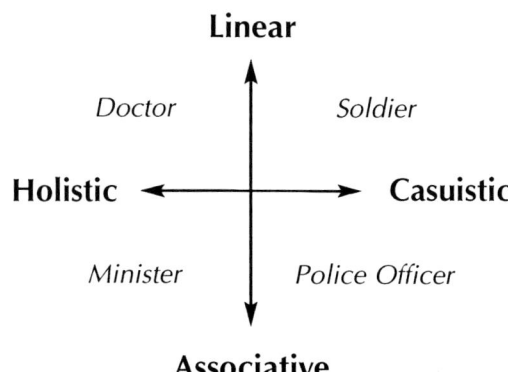

It should be obvious that the best part of this study is using it to make plans for dealing with other people as an effective persuasive communicator. Since there are four poles, there are four polar suggestions; **again, remember that it would be very rare to use any of these entirely as given here. Place each person with whom you will be working on the two parameters of the grid before deciding on a communications strategy;** then you can plan your approach by using the tips below.

LINEAR:
Stay on-task
Don't offer or ask for advice
Work step-by-step
Think "outcomes"
Express opinions directly

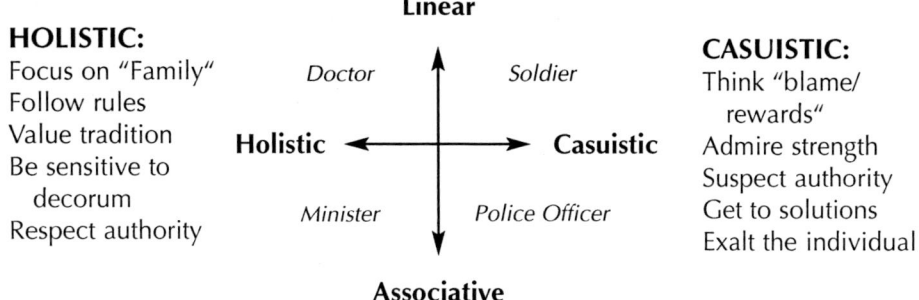

HOLISTIC:
Focus on "Family"
Follow rules
Value tradition
Be sensitive to
  decorum
Respect authority

CASUISTIC:
Think "blame/
  rewards"
Admire strength
Suspect authority
Get to solutions
Exalt the individual

ASSOCIATIVE:
Consider alternatives
Discuss feelings
Express opinions indirectly
Think "process"
Draw in outsiders

The very best part of this tool is that it is both "self-correcting" and "self-directing." You have identified *yourself* as fitting into one of the four quadrants on the basis of your own preferences. You can analyze *other people* by asking the *same* questions, place *them* in a quadrant, **and then honor and respect them by doing any "unnatural acts" described by the "arms" of the grid bracketing their quadrants.** You can get your discussion partner to the right place by *accommodating his or her thought process* and *compensate for its limitations* at the same time. It's not easy—but that's why you get paid the big bucks.

Let's apply this model to the world in which you live.

Chapter 7
Action Activity

As you can guess, the next step will be applying real-world people to the four-step model, by asking two questions. The answers will result in marks falling on each of the two parameters; connecting them will show you the quadrant in which that person falls. From that you will be able to plan your communications strategy. However, before you begin, you need to identify *yourself*, so you will know in what directions *you* need to shift to meet other people.

LINEAR:
Stay on-task
Don't offer or ask for advice
Work step-by-step
Think "outcomes"
Express opinions directly

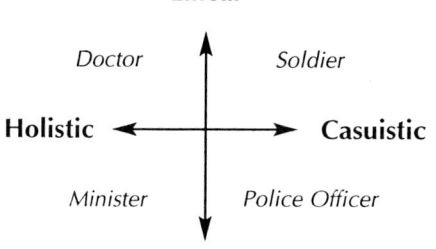

Linear

HOLISTIC:
Focus on "Family"
Follow rules
Value tradition
Be sensitive to decorum
Respect authority

Doctor   *Soldier*

Holistic ⟵   ⟶ **Casuistic**

Minister   *Police Officer*

CASUISTIC:
Think "blame/ rewards"
Admire strength
Suspect authority
Get to solutions
Exalt the individual

Associative

ASSOCIATIVE:
Consider alternatives
Discuss feelings
Express opinions indirectly
Think "process"
Draw in outsider

It also needs to be said that each of us, in our own infinite wisdom (and clear sense of ourselves as MIBU) tend to see all the grand qualities of humankind in ourselves, and consequently place ourselves dead center in such a grid ("That mortal in whom all these qualities bloom—*c'est moi! C'est moi!* It is I!")

Face it—you're wrong. The best way of discovering yourself is by asking the opinions of others—let *them* place *you* on the grid by gauging the 20 points. Then you can do the same with others. And remember—you're looking for answers, not questions.

General Activity

After thoughtful consideration, I have concluded that **my** attitudes toward the issues raised on the grid on the facing page, as perceived by others, result in placing myself at the indicated point on these continua:

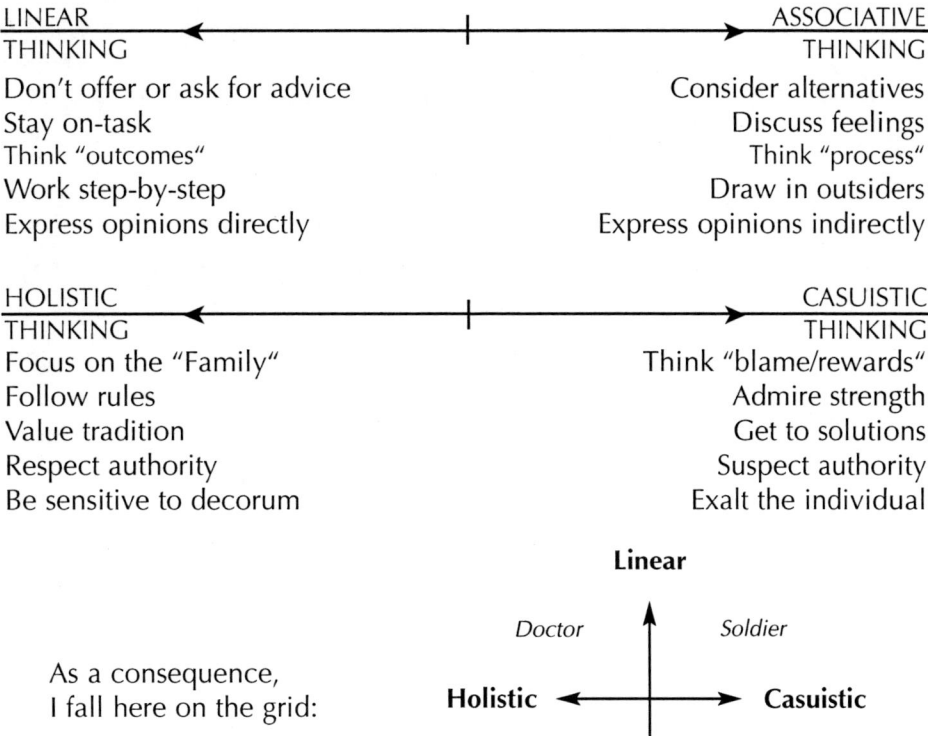

LINEAR THINKING ←———————|————————→ ASSOCIATIVE THINKING

Don't offer or ask for advice	Consider alternatives
Stay on-task	Discuss feelings
Think "outcomes"	Think "process"
Work step-by-step	Draw in outsiders
Express opinions directly	Express opinions indirectly

HOLISTIC THINKING ←———————|————————→ CASUISTIC THINKING

Focus on the "Family"	Think "blame/rewards"
Follow rules	Admire strength
Value tradition	Get to solutions
Respect authority	Suspect authority
Be sensitive to decorum	Exalt the individual

As a consequence, I fall here on the grid:

Linear

Doctor · Soldier

Holistic ←———→ **Casuistic**

Minister · Police Officer

Associative

After further consideration, I have determined that the people with whom I customarily work fall on the grid as follows:

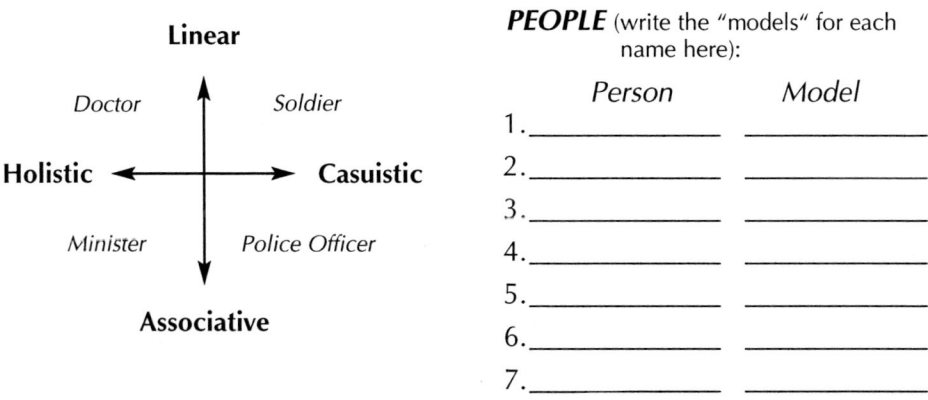

Linear

Doctor · Soldier

Holistic ←———→ **Casuistic**

Minister · Police Officer

Associative

PEOPLE (write the "models" for each name here):

	Person	Model
1.	_____	_____
2.	_____	_____
3.	_____	_____
4.	_____	_____
5.	_____	_____
6.	_____	_____
7.	_____	_____

Specific Activity

Continuing your work on a current or upcoming project of reasonable importance to your and your group's success, which will require you to work with one or more other people, now it is time to complete the cycle of self-discovery by completing the following plan:

Based on the discoveries I have made regarding my own thinking style, and those of the other critical people with whom I work, I have decided to alter my communications style as follows for each individual person with whom I am working on this critical project:

PERSON:

CHANGES I SHALL MAKE IN DEALING WITH HIM OR HER, IN ORDER TO RESPECT HIS OR HER WORLD-VIEW AND INFORMATION-PROCESSING STYLE:

_____

_____

_____

_____

_____

Information Processing Styles Reference

Many readers of earlier editions of this book asked for "quick tips" to help prepare real-world Action Plans, as the ultimate Action Activity. The primary tool for this is the proFILE, of course (see the end of this book); to get you started, following are some vastly oversimplified suggestions on dealing with each of the four main Information Processing styles—the Doctor, the Minister, Police Officer and Soldier. A few suggestions before you start:

- **First and foremost,** always remember that you must use these tools only to honor and respect other people by accommodating their communications preferences and requirements. Your goal is improved relationships, not manipulation (in the bad sense). You are learning how to "do unto other people as they would like to be done by."

- **Second,** the great thing about Cartesian Coördinates is that they allow for variations and subtleties in methods and perceptions. In other words, just because someone were Casuistic, for example, that wouldn't make them a determinist or fatalist; there are degrees of casuistry, and this must be understood and respected as well. The practical consequence of this is that some "Soldiers," for example, will be more extreme in their beliefs than others—some might be "Soldiering Soldiers," for example, while others may be more like Ministers, Doctors, or Police Officers, while still falling generally in the "Soldier" quadrant. And the same could be true for any other quadrant, of course.

- **Third,** as you remember, the key to accommodating other people's needs is matching, not modeling, their personal "Natural feelings." But you must never compromise your own integrity in the process: instead, it is vital that you find ways of meeting the other person on some common ground. Thus, **you** may be a far-left Ministerial Minister, working with a far-right Soldiering Soldier. You can't and mustn't try to pretend to share all those values—but, when working on information-processing, you can try to spot those places where individual responsibility or the need for achieving a quick solution are reasonable (in your own eyes) and stress **those** aspects of the process in your conversation. That will accomplish your goal of accelerating and improving processing without deceit or subterfuge.

So, those are the ground rules. Please use the following with success!

To communicate most effectively with a **Soldier:**

- Clearly articulate goals and methods—use the Turtle
- Keep workgroups as small as feasible
- Be methodical and systematic; use formal team control methods
- Speak directly and clearly about options and opinions
- Consider possible outcomes, consequences, and penalties
- Give personal praise and recognition as appropriate
- Keep excellent records and refer openly to them
- Avoid distractions and interruptions
- Accept responsibility if you make an error

To communicate most effectively with a **Police Officer:**

- Respect and admire strength and authority
- Make sure all affected parties participate in planning
- Be sensitive to others' feelings—explore needs and desires
- Use wide-ranging idea generation methods (brainstorming)
- Let the decision-making process flow freely
- Articulate your opinions indirectly *and ask others for theirs*
- Consider long-term outcomes and consequences
- "Let the chips fall where they may"
- Make sure there is a designated record-keeper

To communicate most effectively with a **Minister:**

- Avoid blaming people; never go *ad hominem* or name-call
- Keep workgroups as large and inclusive as feasible
- Let discussions flow loosely; never *impose* order
- Avoid direct expression of your own opinions; encourage others'
- Always think and talk in terms of "the group's" best interests
- Never rush things—let the process set its own pace
- Be low-key in praising individuals; always thank "the team"
- Make sure records are kept discreetly; don't challenge others
- Observe all social niceties, titles and rituals

To communicate most effectively with a **Doctor:**

- Clearly articulate goals and methods—use the Turtle
- Make sure stakeholder parties are involved in the process
- Be methodical and systematic but don't seem bossy
- Focus on "big pictures"; favor the group over individuals
- Use measurables as benchmarks whenever possible
- Respect leadership roles, titles and privileges
- Speak directly and clearly about options and opinions
- Express the desire to get a decision as expeditiously as possible
- Keep excellent records and refer openly to them

The Information Processing Grid

Linear			
Doctor's Doctor (Surgeon)	Soldering Doctor (Medical Officer)	Doctoring Soldier (Corpsman or Medic)	Soldier's Soldier (Flag rank)
Ministerial Doctor (Medical Faculty)	Policing Doctor (Forensics)	Ministerial Soldier (Chaplain)	Policing Soldier (Military Police
Doctoring Minister (Theologian)	Soldiering Minister (Salvation Army)	Doctoring Police (Internal Affairs)	Soldiering Police (SWAT Team)
Minister's Minister (Missionary)	Policing Minister (Muttawa'a)	Ministerial Police (Social/ field work)	Police Officer's Officer (Cop)
Associative			

Holistic (left axis) · **Casuistic** (right axis)

Most of the information-processing styles you will encounter are clustered around the center of the grid. Subtle differences are important. To identify styles answer the two questions:

Do people think in terms of the *individual* or the *group*?

Do they think in terms of the *process* or the *outcome*?

Now: What will you do with this?

Content:	*What do you want to accomplish?*
Conforming:	*How should you communicate?*
Contact:	*What face-to-face skills will work?*
Control:	*How will you handle circumstances?*
Continue:	*How will you leverage this success?*

Remember—We are all alike, in that each of us is uniquely different.

"It is not the big armies that win battles; it is the good ones."

—Maurice de Saxe

CHAPTER 8: PERSUASION, STEP 2:
GOALS AND GOAL-SETTING

▲ THE WONDERS OF SPAM ▲

"You've got to be careful if you don't know where you're going because you might not get there."
—Yogi Berra

The Rolling Stones told a generation that "You can't always get what you want, but if you try, sometimes, you can get what you need." That may or may not be true; what certainly *is* true is that *you can't **get** what you want until you **know** what you want*. And that is not as easy as it seems. One of the most persistent obstacles to effective persuasion is a lack of a clear vision of expectations (and fall-back positions) on the *communicator's* part. Preventing that obstacle is possible only by adding another step in the process: properly defining **outcomes**.

So, if we want to develop a real-world communications plan that will help us get what we want, the first step must be defining goals and outcomes. This establishes the boundaries of opportunity, so we can begin looking for WIIFMS that will motivate our discussion partner; the **WIIFMS** focus on the *other person* in the communication exchange, just as the **goals** focus on the *purpose* of the exchange.

And, at the same time, we'll decide what our fall-back positions or goals will be, and what we will require from the other person if we modify something we initially desired. In this way, we will prevent problems if we must travel through the *negotiation* stage.

So—with that having been said, how *can* we easily and efficiently define outcomes so we can work toward them? The answer is very simple: we start by recognizing that a goal is not the same thing as a dream or a vision.

A dream is an involuntary vision of something pleasurable, and has the warm and fuzzy look of sleep. A vision is voluntary (we can mold and shape it in our minds), but it is no more concrete than a dream. Both are things that simply would make us happy. The key to understanding them is that we love their very imprecision—as long as the dream or vision is indistinct, we can luxuriate in the thought of having it without ever having to do anything explicit to attain it.

A goal is quite different. A goal is voluntary, as is a desire; however, unlike a desire, a goal can be attained through specific work. The work itself is easy to describe, and conforms to a simple model: it has the attributes of SPAM™.

"SPAM™" is not the same as Spam®, of course. Spam is a processed meat product, named after its ingredients: "**sp**iced **ham**."

SPAM, on the other hand, is an acronym, made up of words that describe the four characteristics of a goal. If something lacks any one of the four, it is a vision or a dream, rather than a goal; if it is not a goal, it is not something you have any reason to think you will obtain. The letters SPAM stand for the attributes

Specific,
Practical,
Actionable, and
Measurable.

The characteristics of SPAM

The first letter in SPAM is "S," which stands for **Specific**. A goal is quantifiable, usually in terms of numbers. For example, "I'd like to lose weight" is a dream or vision; it is imprecise, vague, and unlikely to occur. "I want to lose 5 pounds by the Holidays," on the other hand, is the beginning of a **goal**; it is quantifiable both in volume and time.

Keeping goals quantifiable is difficult, because it pulls us out of our "wish" state and into reality. To do it, just ask yourself, "What limitations would I want on this desire?" For example, if you said "I'd like to lose weight," would you be happy losing 150 pounds? If not, make sure you include the limitation in your goal statement.

The "P" stands for **Practical**. Some goals are unrealistic, and pursuing them would only cause pain. For example, if you want to lose 25 pounds, there is no point in wanting it to take place by this coming weekend—it isn't practical to hope for that. If you want to become a millionaire, you will need certain resources and abilities, which you should consider when stating your goal.

On the other hand, some people with strong goals have achieved them without what would appear to be reasonable abilities—Scott Adams, the author/artist of the Dilbert® comic strip, told himself every morning, as he drew his cartoons, that he would be a famous cartoonist by the time he was 35. The fact that he has virtually no drawing ability should have made his dream impractical—but other gifts pulled him along, and he achieved his goal.

The "A" stands for **Actionable**. This word means that the goal must result from taking a certain step or steps, so you can tell when you are and aren't on track. For example, if you said "I want to lose 5 pounds by the Holidays," you should continue the goal statement by introducing one or more actions. Your goal statement might become, "I will lose 5 pounds by the Holidays, through a combination of cutting out half of the fats in my diet, cutting my alcohol consumption in half, and walking two miles every day."

The actions need to be practical, too, of course. If your goal of losing 35 pounds included the action step of running a 5 minute mile every day—and you haven't run a mile in less than 10 minutes in 30 years—don't bother. You're just heading for disappointment.

Finally, the "M" stands for *Measurable*—and more than the measurements of the "S." "M" stands for *Measurable in incremental steps*, because you need to have benchmarks to indicate progress toward your goal so you can correct shortfalls along the way. Of course, the "A" *Actionable* component helps here; you know what you are supposed to be doing, and you can test whether or not you are living up to your expectations. But you need to keep track of *consequences* along the way, too—and that's easier if you set up signposts.

So your goal might be stated like this:

"I shall lose 5 pounds in the 10 weeks between now and the Holidays, at the rate of $1/2$ pound per week. I shall do this by eliminating half the fat in my diet in every meal, and cutting my alcohol consumption in half. I shall exercise by walking an average of 2 miles a day, at the rate of 4 miles per hour, and shall not miss more than 2 days of exercise in any given week. And I shall not take up any new bad habits between now and reaching my goal that will prevent me from getting what I want."

The chances of fitting into that great Holiday outfit are very good at this point.

SPAM Fall-backs

Remember, "You can't always get what you want, but if you try, sometimes, you can get what you need." This is an important truth, because defining our fall-back positions allows us options and opportunities to keep us out of a simple "success/failure" mode. It's far better to have a range of possibilities with the extremes ("Absolute success" and "Dismal failure") at the ends, and a number of intermediate steps—"Pretty Good," "Not Bad," and "Better than Nothing," for example—in between.

When describing these steps, you use the SPAM model again. And you *always build in acceptable gains to compensate for any possible losses*. For example, if you are negotiating to buy a car, and you establish as part of your goal "I shall not pay the dealer more than $500 over invoice," you are painted into a corner. If, on the other hand, you say, "I shall not pay the dealer more than $500 over invoice *unless s/he does one or more of the follow-*

ing things, each of which is worth $100 to me..." you can get into a win/win situation at the end—even if you wind up paying $700 over dealer invoice.

What go into your lists of possible compensations? Anything that legitimately matters to you. In the preceding example, for instance, you could list any of the following as acceptable trade-offs:
- 1/2% lower financing
- Pin striping thrown in (which costs the dealer less than you)
- Delivery by a certain date
- Extended warranty at the dealer's cost

These are things that you don't want enough to build into your base goal, but they have sufficient value that you would accept them as compensation for a trade-off. And—if in the process of establishing this list you discover something that you really *do* want—you can modify your goal statement *before* you sit down with the dealer.

Thus, your final plan before going into a session as an effective persuasive communicator might sound something like this:

"I want, by the end of the meeting this afternoon—which should be over by 4:30—to have used my color boards and sample books to convince the members of my team to adopt the carpet grade *Biloxi*, in the color *Gris*, for the ground, executive, and Actuarial floors of the project on which we are working; I shall start by convincing Marty, who agrees with me about the color scheme, then get Murat on board, and then get them to help me persuade Sandy, the project leader.

"If they don't agree with me about the Actuarial floors, and give those to an alternative product, I shall ask to have the main lobby done in a custom rug, using *Biloxi* there as a basis, or I shall ask for the Communications department.

"If they don't like the color *Gris*, I shall propose *Amarillo* instead; in that case, we'll shift to the Steelcase furniture.

"If we cannot complete the decision-making by 4:30, I shall propose breaking the project into floor-by-floor steps, and getting commitment on each of them individually today rather than striving to complete the meeting as a whole."

From this, a successful day can emerge.

Chapter 8
Action Activity

This will provide both practice in and application of SPAM skills.

General Activity

For practice, convert the following dreams and visions into SPAM goals:

Dream or vision: *I'd like to make a lot more money.*

SPAM Goal:

Specific   _____

Practical   _____

Actionable   _____

                    _____

Measurable in incremental steps: _____

                    _____

                    _____

Dream or vision: *I would like to be the kind of person who does good things for my fellow humans.*

SPAM Goal:

Specific   _____

Practical   _____

Actionable   _____

                    _____

Measurable in incremental steps: _____

                    _____

                    _____

Specific Activity

Return to the current or upcoming project of reasonable importance to your and your group's success upon which you have been practicing so far. Restate it as a *goal*, conforming to the **SPAM** model.

Original Goal: _____

_____

_____

Goal restated in the SPAM Model:

SPAM Goal:

Specific   _____

Practical   _____

Actionable   _____

_____

Measurable in incremental steps: _____

_____

_____

Using the same model, indicate what your *fallback positions* will be—**specific** things you are willing to lose, and **specific** compensations you must gain to make the losses acceptable. Look especially for offsets in the areas of *schedule versus cost* and *complexity/customization versus standardization*. List the options from *most* to *least* acceptable:

I can concede the following…   In exchange for the following:

1. _____   _____

2. _____   _____

3. _____   _____

4. _____   _____

CHAPTER 9: PERSUASION, STEP 3: QUANTIFIABLE VERSUS EMOTIONAL OBJECTIONS: SET STATEMENTS

▲　　　DEFUSING DIFFICULT SITUATIONS　　　▲

"In the fight between you and the world, back the world."

—Frank Zappa

▲ QUANTIFIABLE VERSUS EMOTIONAL OBJECTIONS; ▲ SET STATEMENTS

When something goes wrong—and it will go wrong; that's the nature of this fallen and fragmented world—it can happen either for predictable or unpredictable reasons. A good strategist always prepares for as many eventualities as possible, in hopes that a great deal of the planning effort will have been unnecessary, and this certainly is true of the effective persuasive communicator.

Failures can occur for either of two reasons: quantifiable objections, which can be reduced to a logical problem and handled through reason, and emotional ones, which are no less manageable, but which require a different set of tools and attitudes.

Up front, it should be obvious that the better the job of preparation done by a persuader, the less likely it should be for problems of any kind to occur; viewed from the other side of the telescope, if the would-be persuasive communicator has to deal with a significant number of objections, or if they occur a significant proportion of the time, the repair and renewal focus should be placed on the *primary communication strategies and systems*, rather than learning excellent ways of correcting the shortfall. In other words, regard failures and problems as signposts pointing you to the front of this book, rather than the back.

That having been said, what are the quantifiable and emotional problems with which you are likely to deal? There are four quantifiable problems, handled with logic (and certain specific PK_3 tools described in Chapter 12):
Misunderstanding,
Skepticism
Indifference
Perceived Drawback

Since these will be discussed later, let's skip them for the time being. Instead, let's focus on something that often lies *beneath* quantifiable problems, and which those problems often mask. That is the range of *emotional* problems, objections, or difficulties.

Emotional objections can occur for many reasons. They all have in common, however, the same root: *I do not understand what is not like what I want to be; I fear what I do not understand, and I reject what I fear.*

Without going too far afield into psychological questions, let's look briefly at each of these sources of objection, and look at what to do in each eventuality. It is important to catch emotional objections as early as possible in the conversation; usually they follow the sequence outlined above:

we do not understand that which is unlike that which we want to be;
we fear what we do not understand, and
we reject what we fear.

If the persuasive communicator can catch the problem in the confusion stage, all is far from lost; in the fear stage, things get dicey, and by the rejection stage s/he is in deep trouble.

The first, and most fundamental, source of an emotional objection is that we are confused or dismayed by what is not like what we want to be. Notice that this is not the same as not being like what we *are*; that is a larger issue. Rather, each of us carries around a picture of what the world is supposed to look like (which usually is modeled on our *idealized* picture of ourselves or, perhaps, our parents); if something does not resemble it, it is not MIBU.

But it also is very important to realize that what we appear to be to others is not how we appear to ourselves (remember the self-identification exercise in Chapter 5); in fact, we save an especially intense dislike for failures that we suspect we might have; deficiencies in our personal realities as compared to our ideals. Thus, people whose intellects are limited are most likely to call other people "Stupid"; people whose economic situation is precarious are most likely to call other people "Low class" or "Trash," and so on. What those people reject is the thing they fear in themselves.

Therefore, the first rule in handling an emotional objection is very carefully analyzing precisely what we have done to convince the other person that we are not the same as MIBU. If it is something that taps into the other person's darkest apprehensions, we know what to do, and not to do, in the future. Then, when continuing the conversation in an attempt to get back on track, we must avoid the dangerous areas while carefully using the information you have gathered about information acquisition *and* relationship to authority *to model and be accessible to MIBU.*

The second step in the sequence is that we fear what I do not understand. Fear is one of the most limiting of human emotions, which can literally drive us into immobility; for the same reason, it is one of the most destructive forces in persuasive communication—since if someone is unable to move and respond to another person's attempts at changing behavior, no further communication is possible.

Or, even worse, action can be entirely irrational: the "blue monkey" phenomenon is a test in which a monkey is removed from its family tribe, painted or otherwise made to appear different, and returned to the tribe. Since it no longer resembles the idealized self of the rest of the tribe, its own brothers and sisters will kill it in a frenzy of fear and anger.

Fear is based on confusion. When another person becomes fearful, it is very important to become encouraging, and work on the emotional levels of the conversation. It does not matter if the fear is directed at or even caused by us, or whether it is the product of external stimuli—we must do the same things: slow down, remove all pressures, and even change the subject of the conversation for a while if necessary. Be especially sensitive to decision making and information processing styles when handling fear.

Rejection is terminal failure of the relationship. It is a form of barely controlled anger. There are only two things to try, one of which may save the day, and the other of which can save merely your hide.

When rejection and anger take place, not only are communication shut down, but also the very window of information flow that allows communication to take place is lost. There is one tool that can help get things going again; it is called a SET statement. It will not solve the problem, but it can get the people into a place where efforts can be made to try to start solving the problem.

A SET statement consists of three parts, which must be completed exactly, in exactly this order. The letter must spell SET, not EST or (worse) SST. The letters SET, standing for "Support," "Empathy," and "Truth," show the parts of the statement and the sequence in which they occur.

*The first part of a SET statement is a reminder to the other person of the fact that you are there to **S**upport him or her. This takes the form of "Believe me, nothing is more important to me than getting this problem corrected. You are vital to me, and I'll do whatever is necessary to get things right."*

*Then, without pausing, you go to the second part of the SET statement—you tell the person that you **E**mpathize with him/her. **Note: you do not claim to <u>sympathize</u>; that only makes things worse**. Instead you merely acknowledge that s/he has feelings, and that those feelings are OK. You might say something like, "I can tell you're angry, and that's OK—you have every reason to be."*

*Finally, you tell the **T**ruth. Say something like, "We have to get beyond this point, so we can get back on track. What can we do now to restart our dialogue?*

This is the best you can do in a bad situation. At this point, you are no longer in effective persuasive communication—you are in damage control, pure and simple. But if that's where you are, that's where you need to be. Keep swimming.

Of course, all your efforts may be inadequate. Everything may collapse, and you are dead in the water. If this happens, apologize to the other person, lick your wounds, study the reasons for the failure, and return to fight another day.

Chapter 9
Action Activity

This one is a little tricky, since it requires you to imagine future personality mismatches—something away from which most people shy, because of our intrinsic belief in MIBU. It's worth the effort, however.

General Activity

Consider the environment within which you currently work, and the people with whom you deal. Which of the people in that world are likely to have any of the following reactions to you, in your role as an effective persuasive communicator:

People with whom I work who may   Something I could do
feel I am meaningfully unlike them: to combat this condition:

1. _____ _____
2. _____ _____
3. _____ _____
4. _____ _____

People who may see in me something they do not understand:
1. _____ _____
2. _____ _____
3. _____ _____
4. _____ _____

People who may see in me something they dislike or fear in themselves:
1. _____ _____
2. _____ _____
3. _____ _____
4. _____ _____

People who may fear me:
1. _____ _____
2. _____ _____
3. _____ _____
4. _____ _____

People who may tend to reject me:
1. _____ _____
2. _____ _____
3. _____ _____
4. _____ _____

Specific Activity

Consider the current or upcoming project upon which you have been working in this book, and complete the same tough analysis:

People with whom I work who may
feel I am meaningfully unlike them:

Something I could do
to combat this condition:

1. _____   _____
2. _____   _____
3. _____   _____
4. _____   _____

People who may see in me something they do not understand:
1. _____   _____
2. _____   _____
3. _____   _____
4. _____   _____

People who may see in me something they dislike or fear in themselves:
1. _____   _____
2. _____   _____
3. _____   _____
4. _____   _____

People who may fear me:
1. _____   _____
2. _____   _____
3. _____   _____
4. _____   _____

People who may tend to reject me:
1. _____   _____
2. _____   _____
3. _____   _____
4. _____   _____

CHAPTER 10: COMMUNICATIONS, STEP 4: RELATIONSHIPS TO AUTHORITY

▲ SIBLING POSITIONS AND THEIR EFFECT ▲
ON WORLD-VIEWS

"The rejection of authority can sometimes result, paradoxically, in an embrace of authoritarianism. Indeed, it can happen with insidious ease."
—Dinesh D'Souza
(*Atlantic Monthly*, 1991)

Much of the material in this book has been known to social scientists for over 35 years or more; other items are less than 2 months old. In between them is the subject of this chapter, which was first explored by the German psychologist Walter Toman and published over 40 years ago; however, the fourth edition of his book *Family Constellation: Its effects on Personality and Social Behavior* was published in 1993. Therefore, the present subject is both old *and* new.

Toman studied the way people form world-views based on their relationships to others, especially their parents (which, here, will be replaced with "caregivers"), brothers, and sisters. In the last few years other authors have followed in his footsteps, developing and promoting modified theories, some of which even that argue that *only* friends and siblings form a child's world-view, and that caregivers count very little.

A veritable cottage industry of "birth-order books" has burst forth recently, watering down and simplifying Toman's ideas unrecognizably. This book will continue that trend, simplifying Toman's ideas to an almost grotesque level. This is because, at that level—the level of the day-to-day workplace, rather than the professional level of studying the psychologies of healthy and unhealthy adults—these ideas can help you become a more effective persuasive communicator.

Please remember the preceding *caveat*—the following chapter does not represent itself as a comprehensive or accurate review of Toman's work, to which you are urged. Instead, it draws on his ideas, as well as other discoveries of the present author, for you to use in the workplace.

In these simple forms, we can readily see that there are three possible sibling placements: one can be an Eldest, a Middle, or a Youngest. [One can also be an *Only*; this is discussed below, as a sort of "super-oldest.] These are true whether the family is adoptive or birthed.

Notice that the formative process is completed by the child's sixth year; thus, one has a sibling role only if one or more brothers and/or sisters are *within six years of the child in question*. So, in a family in which there is a child, a gap of 3 years, another child, and then—after a gap of seven years—a third child, the first is an Elder, the next is a Younger, and the last is an Only. But if the gap between the second and third child were only 3 years, the children would be an Eldest, a Middle, and a Youngest.

Placement in the family structure confers on a child certain benefits and imposes certain liabilities. (Sex is a factor, too—an older brother with a younger sister have a different relationship than an older sister with a younger brother, but we'll not consider that here.) These affect many parts of life, but here we are concerned only with the child's *relationship to authority—his or her own, and that of others.* Use the following information *only* in that area of consideration, recognizing that many, many other factors (both genetic/hereditary and environmental) go into describing, shaping, and forming a human being. This is only *one* of *many* tools you will use as an effective persuasive communicator.

In the broadest and most general terms, placement in the family structure produces the following models, with the resulting worldviews. The world views are described on a continuum from "good" to "bad" traits; it can be assumed that the present reader of this book, regardless of his or her placement in his or her family, lies at the "good" end of the appropriate continuum, and all other family members fall at the "bad" end of theirs.

Elder children

Eldest children are received into the family as "almost-grown-ups." They are given responsibility and involved in family decisions to a greater degree than other children; they receive more of their caregivers' time, and their concerns, idiosyncrasies, aches and pains receive more attention. They are encouraged to be strong and self-reliant, and often are encouraged to earn money to meet their needs. Their caregivers don't know much about parenting, and make a lot of mistakes, often on the side of excessive strictness; unfortunately, parenting comes without instruction manuals.

Eldest children relate to their siblings by assuming the semi-parental role they are given, once they get over their resentment at having lost their even-more-exalted status as Onlies (which see). They willingly share in helping to bring up their younger siblings, while simultaneously terrorizing them. The siblings, in turn, will respond by doing the opposite of the general behaviors of the eldest: a good-student Eldest might have lackadaisical-student siblings, for example, and *vice versa*. It is especially entertaining to watch an Eldest whose parents were Middles or Youngers; the Eldest often will assume the parental role and take over rearing the younger children.

Eldest children form a complicated view of authority. On the one hand, they have it, so they like it; on the other hand, deep inside they know they are frauds (since they are being treated as if they were adults, but they're really only kids, too). Consequently, the Eldest tends to take authority-type careers, or positions within those careers, while being highly skeptical of the authoritative claims of other people. Be prepared to offer proof when arguing with an Eldest.

Therefore at their best Eldests are strong, reliable, and direct; at their worst, they are bullies, skeptics and tyrants. They make excellent leaders, and require reinforcement from others to do their best. A word that might describe them would be *challengers.*

Middle children

Middles undergo a disturbing shift early in life, greater even than that experienced by the Eldest, who goes from Family Deity to mere Center of Attention. Middles, instead, start out as Youngests (see below for traits); then, suddenly, while in their formative years, shift into a new, uncomfortable role, in which they are neither the trusted Eldest nor the beloved Youngest. They can get lost in the process, and feel nobody is paying attention to them; they also feel betrayed, which translates into many life-changing attitudes. Perhaps the most important is that they learn a special *kind* of self-reliance—one based on making deals and alliances with other people. A Middle, with the help of a willing but largely clueless Youngest, can defeat the evil Eldest, once s/he learns how. They can operate beneath other people's radar, and tend to rear themselves. Many never get over their resentment at being cheated.

Middle children relate to their siblings by learning how to make plans and schemes. They also love being part of a group, and make excellent team players later in life. They are capable of balancing a delicate combination of wanting to be noticed, given attention for themselves and what they do, and enjoying the anonymity of doing what they want while evading the attention of their caregivers and elder siblings. However, since most people crave some degree of attention, middles sometimes choose annoying behaviors *in order to be noticed.*

Middle children base their view of authority on resentment of being taken from the cherished Youngest role by arbitrary fate and their suspicion of their Eldest sibling. They place their allegiance in their younger brothers and sisters—in later life, in their teammates—and try to ignore authority when they can, and find ways to evade it when they can't.

Therefore, at their best Middles are companions, team builders, friends, and rock-solid members of the group; they can build a sense of authority and can be excellent persuasive communicators. At their worst, they are sneaks, hole-drillers, and schemers. A word that might describe them would be *collaborators.*

Incidentally, societies favoring large families by definition have more Middles than Eldests or Youngers. This tends to change the behavior of the society as a whole, giving *it* the characteristics of a Middle child, which exacerbates the effects on individual Middles. The reader is invited to speculate on his or her perceptions of national and international politics in this context.

Younger children

Youngest children usually enjoy wonderful stability. They enter the family as the beloved baby, and (unlike the Eldest and Middle) never have this security challenged. Generally, fewer demands are placed on them than on other children, and more is given to them—especially because, in most families, their growth occurs when the caregivers are enjoying higher income than that of the older children. On the other hand, while they get a lot of love, they get less of their caregiver's time and attention than Eldests (although more than Middles). Their caregivers have been through so much at this point that they are fairly blasé about the Youngest's aches and scrapes, leading to a sort of mutual devil-may-care attitude toward harm and risk. Youngests often are happier than their siblings.

Youngest children relate to their siblings by trusting them, and accepting their leadership, as long as it is accompanied by attention and affection; if not, they retreat to their own worlds. Usually, they learn that the Middle is manipulating them, and the Eldest is lording it over them, which can exacerbate the withdrawal from the siblings and reaffirmation that, after all, their caregivers are their best friends.

Youngest children generally love authority—after all, it is the source from which all good things flow. They are trusting and, when not trusting, unquestioning: that is, they tend to shut out, rather than debate with, things they do not like. And, fundamentally, they are *confident:* they will strike out and take risks. As team members when they have a clear sense of WIIFMS they are unstoppable; they usually expect clear recognition for their accomplishments.

Therefore at their **best** Youngests are the sunshine of a group, who make things work as informed members of a focused band of brothers and sisters, or explorers, who cut new trails; at their **worst,** they are selfish people who demand much time and attention. A word that might describe them would be *Columbuses.*

Only children

Only children are in some ways "super-Eldests." Like Eldests, they often are treated as "Almost-grown-ups," and have responsibility and decision-making involvement. In family structures in which there are two caregivers, they receive at least twice as much attention (or more) than other children, and their concerns, idiosyncrasies, aches and pains are indulged. They, too, are encouraged to be strong and self-reliant, but often they are given more resources than are comparable Eldests, who must work for them. Their caregivers don't know much about parenting, but compensate by having two people doing the work of one.

Their world view is so rarefied that the complex social interactions of larger families seem confused and Byzantine. They tend to be trusting, and can be taken advantage of by other, wilier children. Ultimately, however, they think of their families as the centers of their world views

Only children form a very complicated view of authority. On the one hand, they see the duplicity of other children; on the other, they do not see the fraud and deceptions of their caregivers until long after their formative period is over. Therefore, they see things in stark, simple terms; they trust unquestioningly until they discover they have been lied to, and then it is very difficult—if even possible—to get them to trust the liar (or *perceived* liar—not the same thing) ever again.

Therefore at their best Onlies are strong, silent, trustworthy, and mature; at their worst, they are opinionated, excessively self-reliant, inflexible, and naïve (an explosive combination if ever there was one).

What to do with this knowledge:

The first step, obviously, is determining your own family position. This will tell you a lot about the world you live in, and give you insight into both why you do some of the things you do, and also how you are likely to be perceived by others. (For this part of the exercise, look at the "worst" end of the continuum. Sadly, that's how people are. Except you, of course.)

Next, you need a few guidelines for behavior. These are fairly obvious, and are based on the foregoing. There are nine possibilities, which should be considered from *your* vantage point (since you, after all, are MIBU).

IF YOU ARE A CHALLENGER ELDEST OR AN ONLY, first of all, lighten up. It won't hurt. And whenever you find yourself in a persuasive communication situation, take a few seconds to remind yourself that *you are there to communicate with, not control the other person;* or, if you prefer, remind your self that *victory in a persuasive communication situation is measured by whether or not you get what you wanted, not by whether or not you defeated someone else.*

Specifically: **When you are dealing with another Eldest**, make sure you have lots of proofs to support your point, and present them in the correct communications channel. defer to the other person; take the time to study him/her and be very sensitive to subtle expressions of feelings and opinions—especially body language. Swallow hard and shut up several times each conversation. Learn a couple of short prayers or mantras to recite while you're cooling off.

When you are dealing with a Middle, be prepared to make concessions and deals. Be cooperative; allow the other person to shape the final conclusion. Don't be off-put by what appear to you to be sleazy compromises. You are not MIBU anymore.

When you are dealing with a Youngest, be yourself. Be attentive to the other person's need for attention, but in general you have a complementary match. Just don't overdo it and become a bully.

IF YOU ARE A COLLABORATIVE MIDDLE, take time to understand sibling positions of other people. Make certain not to misread Eldests; they have learned that you two are natural enemies. Be straightforward and direct, never say anything you can't prove, and avoid having to modify your position in the middle of discussions Don't indulge your natural desire to get other people to modify theirs.

When you are dealing with an Eldest, do all the things in the above paragraph in spades. Be extremely consistent and serious. Try hard to have proofs available for any position you want to maintain; if you can't find proofs beforehand, modify your position beforehand.

When you are dealing with another Middle, have fun. Enjoy yourself. Wheel, deal, and try to steal™ [just kidding], or BC&S, D [Booze, cruise, and schmooze, Dude]. You'll both love it.

When you are dealing with a Youngest, control but do not modify your natural inclinations. Be prepared to suggest that there is someone else "out there" that is the adversary to your ideas, and enlist the youngest as your ally. You've been doing it all your life; your feet shouldn't fail you now.

IF YOU ARE A COLUMBUS YOUNGEST, there are two unnatural acts you must perform. The first is to begin with a very clear, SPAM-style goal statement, especially including specific fall-back alternatives. Yes, you're impatient; you don't enjoy all that planning sort of stuff. That's why you need to do it. Second, when you get into the persuasive communication itself, allow other people to get the attention, limelight, and praise that you want. Or, even better, do what is for you a *profoundly* unnatural act and provide those services yourself. You have an especially difficult time when dealing with a Middle, because they want to control you; Eldests do, too, but they can be turned into putty when you work your natural Youngest wiles on them. Essentially, all you need to do is keep saying to yourself, "I may be MIBU, but this person is, too."

When you are dealing with an Eldest, as noted above, you are in your element. Be yourself and you'll be fine—with one exception. Never try to convince an Eldest of something that you don't know backwards, forwards, and sideways. You'll lose big-time if you try. Let serious PK_1 be your guide to PK_2, and PK_3 will take care of itself.

When you are dealing with a Middle, again, you can go with the flow. Here, just keep a very clear eye on your goal, so you don't end up thinking you've succeeded and learning instead that you've been snookered.

When you are dealing with another Youngest, it will feel very strange. You must give the other person what you yourself want—attention, pampering, even babying. If you keep a sharp sense of what *you* want, *and then use that information to tell you what to do for the other person*, you can succeed; if you try to keep those things for yourself you will lose. And remember that someone has to be the driver, making sure that the conversation gets where it's supposed to; that driver has to be you. Again, think SPAM.

REMEMBER! *THIS IS NOT THE WHOLE PICTURE*

The tool you learned here describes only how people *relate to authority.* It does *not* describe the whole person. A *challenger* eldest could have a relaxed, amiable social style, a *collaborative* middle might be numbers-oriented, people-oriented, or anything else, or a *cooperative* youngest could be ambitious, modest or many other things. Don't carry this analysis farther than it's supposed to go—and see Chapter 11 for more.

DEALING WITH COUPLES

One final note: many persuasive communicators have wondered how to handle situations in which there are two or more people of apparent equal standing—a husband and wife, for example, or two partners in a successful firm.

There is a marvelous PK_3 trick that is simplicity itself, based on the fact that successful people in a long-term relationship almost always have developed a reliable power-sharing relationship. The present author has observed that with amazing frequency this power-sharing is based on the individuals' respective sibling positions. In successful relationships, they tend to be *complementary*—that is, the participants come from sibling positions that work well naturally—an Eldest and a Youngest, for example.

Notice that this has nothing to do with individual *age*, and it is independent of traditional *gender roles*. All you have to do is observe, not their behaviors, nor their positional relationships (who is the boss, for example), but rather discover their individual *sibling positions*. Once you know this, you will know who is the person in the dominant decision-making role, and you can position yourself as necessary—and defer as necessary to the decision-maker.

Finally, any reasonable person would want some empirical evidence to support the claims in this chapter. Again, it is essential to remember that this aspect of human personality does *not* stand alone in understanding others. Rather, the relationship of an individual to his or her developmental years, and the resulting outlook on experience is part of a whole. If this were not true, it would be easy to predict success or failure based on sibling positions. In fact, the opposite is true. Consider the following:

- Franklin Delano Roosevelt, Laura Bush and Bill Clinton were reared as Onlies, as was Al Gore (his sister Nancy was 10 years older); Mohammad was reared as an Only (and orphaned at 6). Siddhartha Gautama (the Buddha) is reported to have been reared as an Only, although history is murky. At any given moment, about 85% of the students at Harvard are Onlies and Eldests.

- George W. Bush, Albert Einstein, "Jimmy" (James Earl) Carter, Ludwig von Beethoven, Karl Marx and Hillary Clinton were reared as Eldests. Golda Meir was reared as an Eldest (sister Sheyna was nine years older); George Washington also was reared as an Eldest (because of the arrangements for the education of his siblings) and John Adams (the second President) actually was an Eldest.

- Jesus was reared as an Eldest (or an Only, depending on one's beliefs and traditions).

- Napoleon Bonaparte was reared as the second of eight children (a Middle). Lady Diana of England, Martha Stewart, Michelangelo, "Nikolai Lenin," Thomas Jefferson and Dale Earnhardt were Middles as well. John Kennedy was a Middle; his elder brother was killed when he was an adult. Bobby Kennedy (JFK's brother) also was reared as a Middle—the seventh of nine. Rembrandt was the eighth of nine. Ernest Rutherford ("the father of nuclear energy") was the fourth of twelve.

- Mother Teresa was a Middle of five, but her younger siblings died early, so she was reared as a Middle/Youngest, with all the uncertainties that would imply.

- Ronald Reagan was reared as a Younger (of two), as was Friedrich Schiller; Johann Sebastian Bach was the youngest of four. Bill Gates was reared as a Youngest (his sister, Libby, is nine years younger than he). Eva Peron and Mahatma Gandhi were Youngests.

- Moses was born a Youngest (after Miriam and Aaron, his half-brother) and reared in a combination of that environment and that of an Only.

In other words, happiness, achievements, and even power can be enjoyed by people of any sibling position—all that differs is **how** the successes are earned and maintained.

A SUMMARY

Some words to describe ELDESTS:

Sweaty overachievers; accustomed to giving instructions and having a position of leadership; suspicious of other's authority; dislike opposition; fear manipulation and dishonesty; expect to be followed.

Assertive Responsible Independent	Strong-willed Conservative	Reliable Outspoken Challenger	Overbearing Domineering Defiant	Tyrannical Bully Selfish
Accepts authority	Questions authority	Works within authority	Excessively enjoys authority	Fights authority

Some words to describe MIDDLES:

Suave arrangers; accustomed to making plans and deals; seek to overcome, evade or assume authority; dislike inflexibility and authoritarianism; fear being ignored or lost; expect to prevail.

Affiliative Strategian Facilitator	Planner Invisible Negotiator	Developer Organizer Collaborator	Complicated Pushy Manipulative	Amoral Traitor Devious
Supports, helps authority	Deals with authority	Evades authority	Resists and fights authority	Subverts authority

Some words to describe YOUNGESTS:

Sparkling receivers; accustomed to dealing with things; often brave and confident; either like/accept or desire to assert position of authority; dislike insensitivity; fear not being appreciated or respected, expect attention, support and recognition.

Natural Adventurous Cheerful	Attractive Tactician Helpful	Supportive Team player Coördinator	Demanding High-maintenance Low-energy	Spoiled Irresponsible Selfish
Responds well to authority	Likes, uses authority	Understands authority	Expects things from authority	Takes over authority

ONLIES are "super-ELDESTS..."

Except that their lack of experience with deceit and false authority makes them idealistic and vulnerable to manipulation and abuse. They also tend to be high-achievers and prone to judgementalism—often badly aimed.

Approaches for CLOSES:

Oldest/Onlies: Words like *responsibility, authority, "long-term benefit"*; Middles: *best deal, opportunity, "Just for you"*; Youngests: *excitement, rewards, "You've earned it.*

Chapter 10
Action Activity

By now, you have a good idea of the opportunities in this system. As usual, you can now apply the skills described in this chapter to your real-world work life in these exercises. It goes without saying that the effective persuasive communicator doesn't do this sort of exercise once: instead, repeating these evaluations each time your situation—or you—change will help produce a world in which you, and the people around you, achieve the greatest possible happiness of which you are capable of supporting. Obviously, as noted before, you can use these methods for good or ill; both Osama bin Laden and Winston Churchill learned them early, and the results varied greatly. Your perception of "good" and "bad" results will vary depending upon your opinion of these two men; that's OK, too.

General Activity

Consider the environment within which you currently work, and the people with whom you deal. Discover their sibling position, compare it to your own, and decide upon your persuasion strategy here:

My sibling position: _____

My associates' sibling positions:	*The authority role I should assume:*
1. _____	_____
2. _____	_____
3. _____	_____
4. _____	_____
5. _____	_____
6. _____	_____
7. _____	_____
8. _____	_____
9. _____	_____
10. _____	_____

Specific Activity

Now perform the same evaluation for the people involved in your current or upcoming project of reasonable importance:

The project: _____

The goal, expressed in SPAM terms:

_____

_____

_____

The people and our relationships:

My sibling position: _____

	My associates' sibling positions:	*The authority role I should assume:*
1.	_____	_____
2.	_____	_____
3.	_____	_____
4.	_____	_____
5.	_____	_____
6.	_____	_____
7.	_____	_____
8.	_____	_____
9.	_____	_____
10.	_____	_____
11.	_____	_____
12.	_____	_____

This exercise is continued on the next page.

Over your life and career, you have had the experience of working with many people. Some of them were people with whom you "clicked," and always seemed to fit together; with others, each encounter led to various sorts of discomfort.

If you know or can determine the sibling positions of one or more of these people, and compare them to your own, you may discover an important insight into your own psychological needs, and those of other MIBUS walking with you upon the surface of this spinning sphere of rock and mud.

If you are open to a small voyage of discovery, use the space below to record the answer to the following introspection: *Someone with whom I always have had a **bad** relationship was _____, and upon reflection I now realize that part of our relationship was based on the following sibling positions:*

_____

_____

_____

_____

_____

_____

*Someone with whom I always have had a **good** relationship was _____, and upon reflection I now realize that part of our relationship was based on the following sibling positions:*

_____

_____

_____

_____

_____

_____

CHAPTER 11: PERSUASION, STEP 4: INFORMATION ACQUISITION (2)

▲ EYE MOTION AS A CHANNEL-READING TOOL ▲
AND SHE QUESTIONS

"To understand the nature of the people one must be a prince, and to understand the prince, one must be of the people."

—Niccolo Machiavelli

In Chapter 4, we learned that there are three methods by which people acquire information—visually, auditorially, or experientially—and that providing information in the appropriate acquisition channel greatly increases the likelihood of getting it across. And, of course, we have been learning throughout this book that effective *communication* is essential to any sort of effective *persuasion*.

With that having been said, it is time now to learn that the lesson in Chapter 4 was packaged to meet the present reader's need for information in a way that was not overwhelming: now, it can be revealed that there are not three, but rather *seven*, methods by which information is acquired. Readers will be ready to keep on reading; hearers will want an explanation, and experientials will want something to do—all of which follow.

The seven learning methods are variations on the original three. They exist because, in addition to having *perceptual* preferences, our brains appear to be hard-wired in different ways to select various *sorts of content* from the perceptions. These content preferences derive from the sorts of activities we enjoy pursuing, so that the type of *work or hobby we enjoy* both *is formed by* and *forms* the world we perceive, and how we perceive the world.

Thus, people who primarily acquire information through their *eyes* can do so in any one of three preferred *methods*, which are **seeing words**, **seeing numbers**, or **seeing pictures**. Readers and writers fall in the first camp, mathematicians in the second, and visual artists in the third.

People who primarily acquire information through their *ears* can do so in either of two preferred *methods*, which are **hearing stories and narratives**, or **hearing about facts and detail**.

Finally, people who primarily acquire information through *experience* can do so in either of two preferred methods, which are through **personal experience,** or through *observed* experiences of others.

And there is one more new element to this study. In Chapter 4, we learned that we can discover another person's primary information acquisition channel by listening to the words they use. A few moments' reflection should reveal that this is the method of *discovery* that would be preferred by *auditory* people, and that there should be methods of discovery equally biased to seers and feelers. There are, and this is one of the neatest PK_3 tricks of all.

For example, experiential people can use their own bodies and feelings to tap into other people's communication styles. Like Chrissie Hynde's waitress (in "Brass in Pocket"), your "cat moves" will both transmit and encourage the receipt of information about other people's communication channels. And indeed, anyone can learn to use body language as a way of understanding other people. The primary "vocabulary" of body language is the shoulders, hands, and head; the way you "hear" the language is by initiating a conversation with your own body.

Shoulders are windows into a person's level of interest in and involvement with another. Shoulders bunched together or pointed toward the other person are barriers, and indicate broken communication; open, relaxed shoulders indicate an exchange or relationship. If you are experiential—or want to test for an experiential character in another person—relax your shoulders while making eye contact; resistance indicates that the other person doesn't feel that it's time to proceed.

Hands are an excellent indicator of whether or not the other person is experiential. The obvious clues are touching and caressing—of a product, a surface, or an arm or sleeve; the experiential does it, and others are less likely to. If someone touches something, look to see whether they act as if they are enjoying it—if so, they probably are experiential. Many experientials can't control themselves when they discover something interesting—they will reach out and take it away from the other person.

Less obvious, but still very important, clues lie in how the person holds and moves his or her arms and hands. As a general rule, people move their hands out to the edge of their personal "privacy zone"; this both warns other people not to approach too closely, and reveals the person's perceived size or required space. As a rule of thumb, experientials will have larger spaces than other people, and yet appear to invite other people into their zones. Visual people, on the other hand, use the edges of their privacy zones as barriers; when given something to examine they will hold it out to the edge of the zone so as to examine it in a better light or as a whole.

If you are an experiential—or are acting as if you were one—use these tools to understand others. Moving in and gesturing as if to touch the other person quickly will reveal whether she or he is experiential, or (at least) relates to you as experiential. Holding something at the edge of the other person's space and watching to see whether or not s/he takes it is another good clue. And—perhaps most important of all—*matching movements of the body*—will build rapport, especially with experientials.

Here's how that skill works: let's assume that you are speaking to another person, and you move slightly toward him or her. S/he either is not experiential, or for some reason does not welcome you into his or her private space, and therefore moves away slightly. You now have two choices: move in again, so you can chase the other person backwards around the room (sending a clear "we're different and I don't like you" message), or stay where you are, outside your own comfort zone—with the other person still having made an unanswered "escape" move. Neither possibility advances the cause of persuasive communication.

Now, instead, let's assume that in response to your advance, the other person moves away and you reply by **moving *back* yourself**. If you have moved farther from his or her comfort zone than she or he likes, s/he will then *move towards you*. In this case, the subliminal message is that s/he wants to be closer to you—a message you want to endorse.

If you carry this forward, you see that the same model works if the other person moves first. If s/he moves toward you, *move very, very slightly toward him or her*. That says, "I want to be even closer to you than you do to me." Then almost immediately, slightly back up to the original distance. Both balance and friendliness will have been established. If the other person moves away, move backward yourself. When s/he reestablishes the original distance, the same messages will have been sent and received.

Finally, there is the head. Experiential people tend to pay less attention to the placement of their heads than do visual or auditory people, for obvious reasons—their heads are not the repositories of their primary information acquisition organs. Visual people, on the other hand, look at things intently, and can even seem to be staring, pointing their heads at the subject of their interest; auditory people tend to cock their heads when listening, as if to aim their ears, and often try to make eye contact with the speaker with their eyes at an oblique angle (while the visual people will turn their heads to maintain direct contact). If you are an experiential person, that's OK; you probably won't be noting the other person's head motion at all. However, you will know everything there is about his or her hands. And this leads to one of the most interesting studies of all: the way *visual* people can read other people's communication styles.

Just as auditory people listen for verbal clues, and experiential people use the feelings derived from their bodies and hands, visual people can gather information about communications channels by **watching other people's eyes**. To do this, you need to have a specific type of prepared question that will encourage the other person to pause and reflect upon the answer. While he or she thinks, his or her eyes will do one of three things, and this will reveal his or her preferred channel. Using this tool requires a specific type of question called a *SHE* **Question**.

A SHE question meets three criteria: it is a question about a
    Specific
    Historical
    Event.

In other words, a question such as "What were the reasons you bought your first car, and what do you remember about it?" is a SHE question. It asks about something that was an *event*—a memorable purchase—that was tied to a *specific* object in the *historical* past.

Another SHE question is, "How did you acquire the carpet that's in your house right now? What do you like and dislike about it?"

It's important not to "load" the SHE question in the direction of one of the information acquisition channels. For example, "What did your first car look like?" would give visual information, regardless of the other person's preferred channel; "How did you feel on your first date?" biases the answer for feelings.

Whatever the SHE question you ask, you do two things when the

other person replies: first, obviously, you listen to the words they use in their answer; those words will reveal what something looked like, or what people said about it, or how they felt when they used it. That will be a big clue for their learning channel. *At the same time, you watch their eyes. Their eyes will do one of three things: look up, look to one or both sides, or look down and to their right*. This will reveal the other person's information acquisition channel.*

If, in response to a SHE question, the other person *looks up*, s/he is searching for a blank surface on which to project the picture of his or her memory. This is the hallmark of someone who prefers to *acquire information visually.*

If the other person *looks to one side*, or from side to side, s/he is asking for help from his or her most trusted ally: the ears. Sideward, or side-to-side, motion identifies a person who *likes to acquire information audially.*

If the other person *looks down and to the right*, at the hand associated with work in most cultures, s/he is revealing confidence in doing and feeling. Eye motion down and to the right reveals someone who *prefers to acquire information experientially.*

Eye motion down and to the left has another possible meaning, described below. If you encounter this, another method is used to determine this person's preferred information channels.

Can someone's preferred information-gathering channel change? Absolutely. Often, it even changes several times during a conversation, as different aspects of the subject are examined. *As long as you are watching eye motion and listening for key vocabulary, you will know where that person is, and be able to respond with information in the best possible way at each precise moment.* As we observed in Chapter 4, this will make certain that you are where the other person needs you to be, before they even realize that's where you are going.

With the basic discovery made, how can you distinguish between the seven subtypes—the *seers* who prefer **words**, **numbers**, or **pictures**, the *hearers* who favor **stories and narratives** as opposed to those who like **facts and detail**, and the *experiencers* who learn from **their own** or **others'** histories?

The first tool is simple comparison of the people with the demands of their jobs. Assumptions are always dangerous, and must be tested against reality; they are a great help in speeding up the process of getting to the truth, however, as long as they are understood to be *hypotheses* rather than *facts*. Thus, one can make *and then test* the assumption that an architect is a picture-visual, an accountant a number-visual, and an author a word-visual; a stories-and-narratives-hearer a "people" person and a "facts-and-detail-hearer a "problem-solver" type, and so on.

Observation provides a second method of making the determination. Notice whether the other person habitually uses pictures, charts, testimonials, spoken facts, or other methods when *s/he* is working on persuading *other people.* The method that s/he uses is almost certainly the one in which s/he is most naturally comfortable (assuming that s/he is not skilled in and using the same methods as you are now learning, of course).

Perhaps the best way of testing (and an excellent way of verifying your hypothesis) is a combination of the two specific tools you have already learned: asking a SHE question, watching for eye motion, and then listening for *detail* in the reply. For example, a picture-visual will look upward and then describe an image in concise but precise detail, while a word-visual will look upward and then provide information at greater length, and with more dramatic flair. The experiencer who learns from his or her own actions will look down and to the right and tell you how s/he felt during the experience, and what it meant to him or her; the experiencer who learns from others' actions will tell you about the feelings and experiences of his or her friends or associates.

What use will you make of this knowledge? It's pretty self-evident. Whenever you make a presentation to, or engage in a conversation with, another person in order to be an effective persuasive communicator, take the time to understand the other person's information acquisition needs and place the information you offer in the precise style best suited to ensure that the other person receives it. A few simple and obvious rules of thumb are as follows:

For the **Visual** *person who is sensitive to* **pictures***:*
>Use lots of pictures.
>Hold samples up for him/her to see.
>Present data in graphs and other pictograms.
>Pay attention to your appearance.

For the **Visual** *person who is sensitive to* **words***:*
>Have letters and testimonials.
>Give him/her copies of all written materials to keep.
>Present data in charts and graphs.
>Make generous use of written guarantees.

For the **Visual** *person who is sensitive to* **numbers***:*
>Use pictures carefully and precisely.
>Make moderate use of samples.
>Present data in tables and written testimonials.
>Don't be distracted by his/her seemingly random body language.

For the **Audial** *person who is sensitive to* **narratives***:*
>Tell lots of anecdotes.
>Encourage him/her to talk by using open probes.
>Use written materials very, very sparingly; tell your story.
>Pay attention to his/her body language.

For the **Audial** *person who is sensitive to* **facts and detail***:*
>Have lots of data and facts that you can recite smoothly.
>Pay very careful attention to your speaking style.
>Prepare answers for most of the likely questions.
>Have stories about savings and other measurable consequences.

For the **Experiential** *person who learns from* **personal** *events:*
>Always keep something in his/her hands.
>Make sure s/he has something physical to take away.
>Check early on to see whether touching is necessary.
>Keep moving.

For the **Experiential** *person who learns from* **others'** *events:*
>Always keep something in his/her hands.
>Model behaviors you want him/her to follow ("Walk this way").
>Do lots of demonstrations; *invite* him/her to participate.
>Be prepared to spend a long time in the conversation.

And in this way, you will become ever-more persuasive. On the following pages is a summary of the ideas in this section.

The Visual Communicator

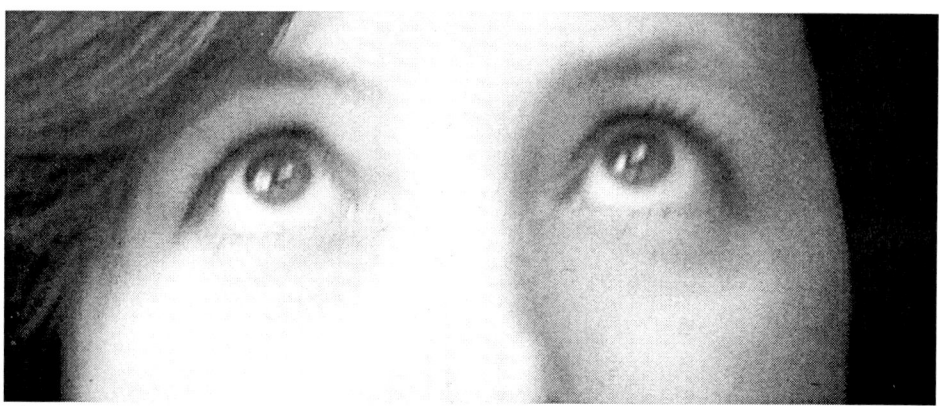

Hallmark: Looks upward when thinking

VOCABULARY: words like "see, picture, view, and look."

HOW TO PRESENT TO VISUALS: Hold things up for him/her to see. Use good lighting. Have lots of handouts and pictures. Allow him/her time to read and study. *Don't interrupt him or her while (s)he is reading.* Be quieter and less assertive than usual; if you are an Audial, speak only when spoken to.

PROOFS: Charts, graphs, letters, data (as appropriate for each individual. Some Visuals like pictures, and others like numbers. Look for clues.)

CONTACTS: Write; don't phone. Be concerned about your appearance, and pay attention to his or hers: restrained and perceptive compliments usually are suitable. Look for visual clues in the workplace, and comment on them as appropriate. Visit sparingly. Don't touch unless initiated by him/her.

The Audial Communicator

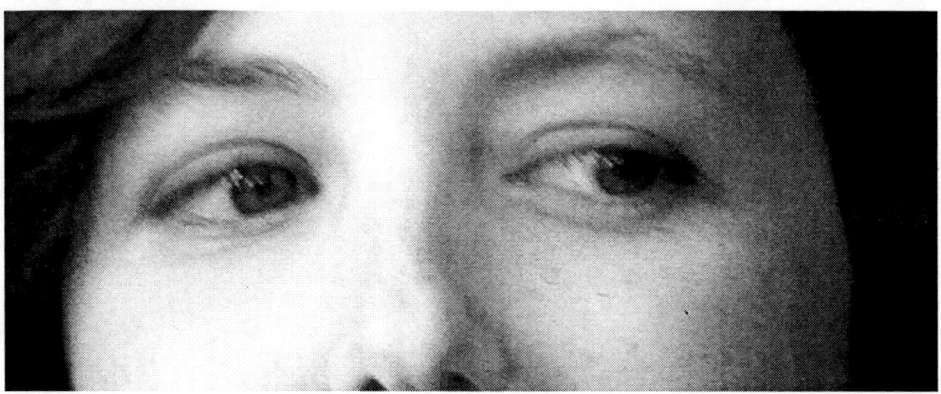

Hallmark: Looks to one side or other when thinking

VOCABULARY: words like "hear, tell, story, listen."

HOW TO PRESENT TO AUDIALS: Have lots of stories about how things have performed. Offer phone numbers of people to call for references. Practice your presentation, so that it will sound polished. Don't "hem" or "um." Allow lots of time when you visit.

PROOFS: Anecdotes, testimonials, third-party endorsements; verbal summaries of test results. Don't assume that Audials only want fluff; make sure that your stories include facts. The ARTS CD recordings and audio tape version of *Trade Secrets* are excellent examples of your company's commitment to doing things "Right the First Time"; even though they aren't strictly relevant, Audials respect the spoken word and the companies that produce them

CONTACTS: Phone and visit a lot, and tell more stories when you do. Tell jokes when you get the chance, if you can. *Listen attentively and respond with clear Support Statements.* Shut up when s/he is talking, but respond quickly when s/he finishes.

The Experiential Communicator

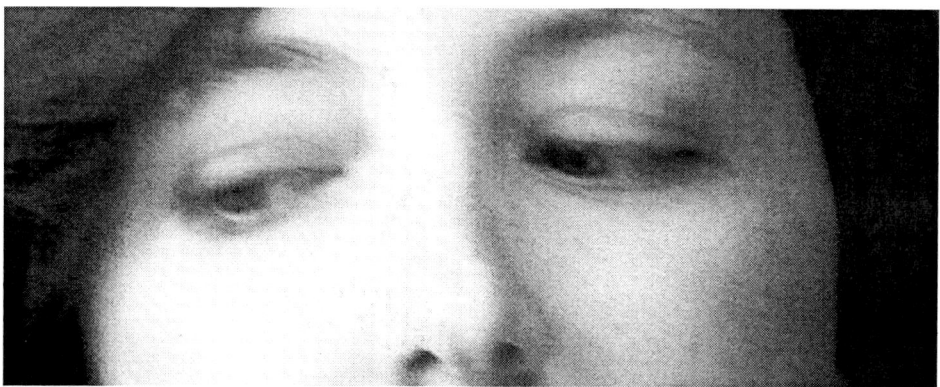

Hallmark: Looks down and to the right when thinking

VOCABULARY: words like "Feel, handle, pride, sensation, work."

HOW TO PRESENT TO EXPERIENTIALS: Let him/her hold things. Get him/her involved—draw, compute, move around. Experientials tend to have shorter attention spans than Visuals (who have the longest) and Audials; keep each aspect of your presentation short, and try to be done in 24 minutes at the most. (Spend no longer than 7 minutes on any one subject.) If you are showing product, make certain there is a small piece for each Experiential to hold, and keep if possible; don't ask them to pass things around, because you will lose their attention totally while that is going on.

PROOFS: Do things together; invite him or her to visit an installation, for example. Give him or her samples to play with and (if performance claims are an issue) destroy. Make a point of the fact that you are working hard for him or her (Visuals and Audials don't care). Never seem to be lecturing or talking down to an Experiential.

CONTACTS: Don't write or phone if you want to be taken seriously—visit. Touch. React. Live, love, laugh and be happy.

Blocking

Hallmark: Looks down and to the left when thinking

"DANGER, Will Robinson!"

Up to this point, we have considered only three types of eye motion: up, to either side, or down and to the right. Obviously, there is a fourth possibility: moving the eyes down and to the person's *left*. This motion indicates blocking—"Reptile Brain" editing of processed information. The person with whom you are dealing is involuntarily keeping information from himself or herself, which is *not* the same as lying (about which please see the next page). If you encounter this eye motion, *leave the subject at once* and change topics.

About Things that Are Not So

Often, when the subject of reading eye motion to discover communications channels comes up, questions about the words "shifty-eyed" follow along, and the discussion of *blocking* exacerbates those questions. This is of more than a little importance, first to assist the salesperson/communicator in providing information, and second to prevent *two* potentially dangerous misunderstandings.

The first misunderstanding: People who use the audial mode—those who look to the side when thinking—*are not any more inclined to dishonesty than other people.* They simply use their ears to gather information. *However, the converse is **not** true:* **when people are lying, they usually are in the audial mode.** This is because they must remember what they said before. Additional kinemes that indicate lying are unusual stress in the voice and hand motions that either cover or distract from the mouth—as if to say, "pay no attention to my words, because they are false."

The second misunderstanding is that "blocking" and "lying" are the same. They are not. *Blocking* is keeping information *from the speaker himself or herself.* Frequently, this means that unpleasant details are being suppressed. For the effective communicator, the rule is simple: use blocking as a warning to leave the subject, and "shifty" eye and hand motion to alert you to the possibility of duplicity.

The aid to communications. The tendency to cover the mouth and avert the eyes in response to dishonesty is so strong that *some people make this kineme in response to what they perceive to be dishonesty in other people.* If you are speaking to someone else, and while you speak *the other person displays the aversion kinemes,* consider the possibility that you are perceived as lying. Frequently, this is merely the result of using an inappropriate communications channel; for example, if you present accurate information to a visual person, and you use experiential channeling, the customer may respond with the "dishonesty perception" kinemes. In that case, *verify what you are doing and change course.*

And, obviously, if you are telling the truth and using the right channel, you have another problem on your hands—it's called skepticism.

These tools will serve you well. Use them with success!

Kinesics at Work

Photo by Diana Walker © 1998 Time Magazine

"I am going to say this again. I did not have sexual relations with that woman, Miss Lewinsky."

—William Jefferson Clinton,
President of the United States,
Television interview,
26 January 1998

Among the signals involuntarily sent during this interview, three—the linguistic stress markers and the two kinemes (the eyes to the side, and the distracting finger waving)—form a cluster that clearly suggest concealment or dishonesty.

Chapter 11
Action Activity

These activities are more theoretical than the previous ones, because we are getting farther and farther from your previous experiences and more into what probably is fairly new knowledge; therefore, they are both more *difficult* and more *necessary* than the earlier ones. Please don't succumb to the temptation to skip them.

General Activity

Considering the sort of persuasive communications you normally perform or are likely to have to perform, what resources are available for you in each of the following categories:

• Pictures (photos, drawings)

_____

_____

_____

• Samples

_____

_____

_____

• Graphs and other pictograms

_____

_____

_____

• Testimonials, both written and oral

_____

_____

_____

• Charts and tables (the terms are intended to mean lists of numbers)

_____

_____

_____

• Written guarantees or promises

_____

_____

_____

• Relevant anecdotes

_____

_____

_____

• Hard data (such as savings and other measurable consequences)

_____

_____

_____

• Things to play with

_____

_____

_____

• Take-aways

_____

_____

_____

Specific Activity

Returning again to the current or upcoming communications project upon which you have been working in these exercises, list the specific resources you have and, on that basis, determine what you need to acquire, given the information acquisition styles of the people with whom you will be working:

The project: _____

People with whom I shall be working on this project:	*What their communications model requires:*	*How I will meet each of those needs:*
_____	_____	_____
	_____	_____
	_____	_____
_____	_____	_____
	_____	_____
	_____	_____
_____	_____	_____
	_____	_____
	_____	_____
_____	_____	_____
	_____	_____
	_____	_____
_____	_____	_____
	_____	_____
	_____	_____

CHAPTER 12: COMMUNICATIONS, STEP 5: DECISION-MAKING

▲ AMIABLES, EXPRESSIVES, DRIVERS, AND ▲
ANALYTICALS, AND
THE FIVE WAYS OF ACHIEVING COMMITMENT

"It is the nature, and the advantage, of strong people that they can bring out the crucial questions and form a clear opinion about them. The weak always have to decide between alternatives that are not their own." (Es ist der Vorzug und das Wesen der Starken, dass sie die grossen Entscheidungsfragen stellen und zu ihnen klar Stellung nehmen können. Die Schwachen müssen sich immer zwischen Alternativen entscheiden, die nicht die ihren sind.")

—Dietrich Bonhoeffer

One of the most interesting—and universally accepted—tools of "casual" psychology that, while accessible, is not mere psychobabble, is the study of *social styles*. "Social styles" are the various predictable ways in which people interact with other people in content-rich situations; for the purpose of the present system of persuasive communications, these social style models are used as a method of controlling the *decision-making* process.

Social style profiling, in one form or another, has been around for about 3000 years. Plato observed that people tend to have one of four dominant *humors* (the word is preserved in our word "humorous," meaning "full of vivacity"); the Platonic humors, as interpreted by Medieval physicians, were phlegm, blood (sang), and black and yellow bile. Again, the concepts have survived; people today still are said to be "phlegmatic," or "sanguine," or "bilious."*

In the United States today, the system is almost ubiquitous: in the US Air Force, for example, people are categorized into four groups—Eagles, Peacocks, Doves, and Owls—and similar systems are used in other arenas. The best known system was popularized by the Meyers-Briggs tests, and those are the terms that will be used here. However, the system used here in identifying people as belonging in one of the four main categories is much, much simpler than the Meyers-Briggs—in fact, it is so simple that it can be employed with less than two minutes of observation, with an accuracy rate greater than 80%.

In case you're interested, the old terms survive to the present day with the following meanings: phlegmatic *now means apathetic, dull, unexcitable, or sluggish;* sanguine *now means cheerful, optimistic, hopeful, or confident, and* bilious *means peevish, irritable, cranky, or unpleasant. In the medieval period, as noted above, bile came in two flavors; black bile was thought to cause gloominess, and yellow bile was associated with irritation or* choler. *This latter distinction survives in the modern word* choleric, *meaning prone to anger. In medieval times, these words had meanings much more positive than they do today; if you've looked ahead in this book, the approximate equivalents of the original meanings of these words, as compared to the contemporary terms, might be* sanguine *is similar to "Amiable" [or Doves];* phlegmatic *is similar to "Analytical" [or Owls];* choleric *is similar to "Driver" [or Eagles], and* bilious *is similar to "Expressive," [or Peacocks].*

The key to using this tool is recognizing that each of us has certain specific reasons for relating to other people as we do and that those reasons usually are based on a wide variety of individual genetic patterns, experiences, and knowledge. Understanding those biochemical underpinnings and specific experiences could take a lifetime, and we don't have that much time to commit to understanding each other person we might want to influence. However, we can short-circuit the situation by dealing instead with the *responses to life* that each of us carries and making communications plans based on the results we *observe* in other people.

There are two ways of discovering these consequential outcomes: one is taking a standardized test (such as the Meyers-Briggs, mentioned above, or any of the dozens of alternative versions) which can take an hour or so to complete and evaluate. And the other is making summary observations of key behaviors and comparing them to a pattern of predictable results. This second method, which produces results in under 120 seconds by completing two simple evaluations, is the one you will learn here.

The core of this method is the fact that, as we have been discussing throughout this book, most normal people want the same kind of thing—the outcomes they prefer and desire—but the specific things they want are as different as the people themselves. This means that all else being equal people will try to influence others, and will do so in two ways: they will either clearly state what they want, or will let others infer their desires from their words and actions, and they will either reveal their own feelings and emotions, or conceal them as being irrelevant, impertinent, or an obstacle to achieving their goals..

This leads to the first of the Three Beautiful Things (TBT) about this tool: *it doesn't matter whether the other person is trying to* **appear** *open or closed, or direct or indirect, (or anything else), or really* **is** what she or he appears to be: *you can provide influence using appropriate tools and techniques, so they can come to the decision they desire.* This is a positive and powerful ability.

The second of the TBTS is equally powerful: *the act of deciding how you and the other person relate* **automatically tells you the behavior changes to make in order to obtain the outcome you desire**—whatever it may be. The model *measures* the behaviors you *desire*. In other words, when you have learned *your own personal* decision-making style, and then have measured the *decision-making style of other people*, and you then desire to honor MIBU by considering *their* style as important as your own, all you have to do is use the parameters of the measurement system as models, *moving your behaviors closer to the other person's by doing the things they desire—according to* your *evaluation.*

As we noticed above, the decision-making process comes down to articulating our desires, and understanding the desires of others, in a clean and comprehensive way. Therefore, we merely need to learn how to evaluate these two desires of other people, placing them on a continuum (to avoid oversimplifying the complexity of the mind of another person) and then comparing those determinations to the same evaluation of ourselves. Then we will know how to proceed.

We do this by answering two simple questions. The first is, **"When it comes time to express opinions, does this person *usually* ask questions that reveal what s/he actually desires, or does s/he more often simply *tell* what s/he thinks should be done?"** And the second question is like unto it, **"Does this person conceal or reveal information about himself or herself when communicating with other people?"**

The first question is not "wimps versus bullies." The issue is *how one approaches the task of making decisions*, not what kind of person is being considered.

Some people prefer to build consensus by starting with other people's desires, holding their opinions back until an appropriate time so as not to influence the discussion, while others feel that the appropriate time is up front, to avoid confusion. Both people *have their own desires*; the issue is merely *how they approach the task of getting what they want*. The desire is constant; the method of attaining it is not. And very few people *consistently* use one method or the other; that's why there is a *continuum* for this question: place the person somewhere *between the extremes*.

And the second question is not "sneaks versus blabbermouths." Some people feel that their personal lives are inappropriate for a given context, while other people feel that interpersonal relationships are the heart of good relationships. Again, the goal is to honor and appreciate people for who they are; again as well, most people fall somewhere on the continuum *between* the extremes.

Which leads to the third, and best, of the TBTS about this tool: it is stunningly, blindingly, stupefyingly, *simple*. It requires *no* complicated measurements, tests, analysis, or resolutions. Just ask two questions of yourself, and as a consequence determine where the other person falls on two continuum lines. Then, when you have determined where the other person fell, you can honor him or her as MIBU by taking the time—and having the concern—to match your closing style at which you ask for commitment to the path or choice you are proposing) in the *style which s/he finds most comfortable, congenial, and appropriate.* That's it.

This is the first question you ask yourself about the person being evaluated. Place a mark on the line indicating where s/he falls:

Compared to others, this person falls where indicated on the continuum of "concealing" to "revealing" personal information:

CONCEALS   REVEALS
SELF   SELF

"Average"

And then ask the second question, again placing a mark to indicate where the person falls on *this* line:

Compared to others, this person falls where indicated on the continuum of first "asking" or "telling" as a way of communicating opinions:

ASK TO   TELL TO
EXPRESS   EXPRESS

"Average"

Then, you transfer those measurements to the lines on this grid:

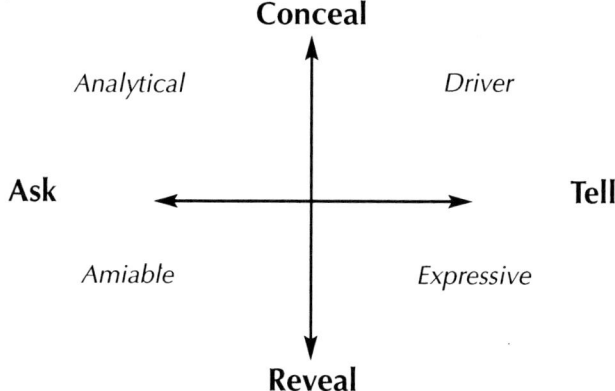

The result—once you draw vertical and horizontal lines from the points on the axes of this grid—indicate the decision-making style of the person being evaluated. People who *reveal* and *tell* are "Expressives"; those who *reveal* and *ask* are "Amiables"; those who *ask* and *conceal* are "Analyticals," and those who *conceal* and *tell* are "Drivers."

The great risk of this system is that those who use it tend to fall in love with the *descriptive words*, and forget to ask the two *revealing questions.*

In other words, someone who is outspoken, boisterous, and friendly might be called an "Expressive" on the basis of those behaviors—but a careful analysis might reveal that s/he was using *loud, extroverted* actions to conceal the fact that s/he was hiding, rather than exposing his or her personal feelings, and that while s/he seemed to be expressing his or her *desires*, in reality the sentences were filled with "What do you think?" questions. In short, this seeming "Expressive"—when analyzed with this simple system—actually was an *Analytical*—the Expressive's polar *opposite.*

Once you have determined the general descriptive category for the decision-maker with whom you are working, you can decide how to proceed. There are two applications: deciding how to *structure your conversation*, and selecting a strategy for *ending the conversation with agreement on a course of action.*

Remember, the second of the TBTS (Three Beautiful Things) of this system is that *all you have to do to be more **appealing** to the other person is do the things that **describe** that person.* Of course, you operate from your own personal comfort level, so once you have placed yourself on the Social Styles Grid (remembering to do this separately for each person with whom you interact, because each person has a different perception of *you*), you adjust by doing things in the *other* quadrants. In general,

---

Drivers should do *less* telling and *more* asking; be *less* concealing and *more* revealing.

Amiables should do *less* asking and *more* telling; be *less* revealing and *more* concealing.

Analyticals should do *less* asking and *more* telling; be *less* concealing and *more* revealing.

Expressives should do *less* telling and *more* asking; be *less* revealing and *more* concealing.

If you want more specific advice to help your matching efforts succeed, here are some tools that have been proven successful. Take them with a grain of salt, of course, and remember that MIBU is a complicated being: there are many other aspects of his or her whole personality that you must understand and to which you must respond.

To increase perceived REVEAL behaviors
(To match Amiables and Expressives)

- Speak openly about your feelings.
- Be sensitive to body language—avoid "closed" positions.
- Engage in casual talk about non-business subjects.
- Pay personal compliments.
- Tell anecdotes about your family; ask about his/hers.
- Invest time in phone calls, notes or visits (as appropriate).
- Arrive early and plan to stay late.
- Use words relating to relationships, sharing, and feelings.
- Don't try to lead the conversation.

To increase perceived CONCEAL behaviors
(To match Analyticals and Drivers)

- Avoid comments about the other person's appearance
- Be business-like and meticulous at all times.
- Stay on the subject. Use written notes whenever possible.
- Dress carefully and neatly, up-scale in the vernacular.
- Don't discuss personal issues.
- Retrain obvious enthusiasm and interests.
- Be punctual: don't overstay your appointed welcome.
- Be brisk, but don't rush through your meeting.
- Show that you are leading the conversation toward a goal.

To increase perceived TELL behaviors
(To match Drivers and Expressives)

- Don't waste time. Get to the point.
- State your opinion clearly and as articulately as possible.
- Be consistent.
- Volunteer information.
- Use Closed Probes freely, making good Support Statements.
- Take the lead when necessary, but watch for his/her desires
- Accept that you may disagree; when it happens, be respectful.
- Use the PK_3 skills freely and extensively.

To increase perceived ASK behaviors
(To match Amiables and Analyticals)

- Use Support Statements freely and correctly.
- Be prepared to negotiate and compromise.
- Listen carefully; show you listen by asking questions.
- Be flexible about meeting times, places, and circumstances.
- Allow the other person to lead some of the time.
- Use Open Probes whenever possible.
- Invite other people to share in the decision-making.

Asking for commitment

The goal of any persuasive system is *achieving agreement on a proposed product or plan*, although (as we have seen) there are many other applications for these tools. But now it is time to get to the goal of effective persuasive communication: commitment.

Asking for a commitment—asking for an *order*, in salespersons' terms—is called *closing*. A close consists of two parts:

- A list of benefits already accepted by the negotiating partner, with a pause after naming each item in the list to allow him or her to nod in agreement that this is a point of congruence, followed by
- A request for commitment, phrased in a method appropriate for the person and situation at hand.

The first step—reciting the list of benefits accepted by the other person—is necessary for three reasons:

- It summarizes the conversation, and alerts the other person to prepare to take an action;
- It sets up a climate of agreement, in which a series of "yes: answers (to Closed Probes to which you already know the answer) leads logically to the answer you want in the Request for Commitment (which is "Yes," in case we've gotten things so muddy that you've forgotten), and
- It actually sets up a neurological change in the brain (called *biofeedback*; the probable mechanism is the "Placebo effect") in which the other person *literally* is primed—that is, fluids are in place to initiate a process—to respond with a positive answer.

The request for commitment can be phrased in any one of five methods, determined by the social or decision-making style of the other person. The five methods—the five closes—are traditionally called by the following names:
- Direct,
- Alternative,
- Step-by-step,
- Assumptive, and
- Positive negative.

Let's look at them in more detail.

The **Direct close** is a simple request for a yes-or-no answer. The upside is that it is short, sweet, and efficient; the downside is that the answer might be "No." Of course, this is far from fatal; if the other person says "No," you simply make an Open Probe, such as "Oh? Could you tell me why?" and keep going.

The **Alternative close** is only slightly less simple. Instead of asking for agreement, you offer two choices, *each of which is equally acceptable to you*, and ask the other person to select from them. You will be satisfied with the reply, and so will the other person. And, of course, if s/he doesn't like either of your choices you Open Probe for more needs.

The **Step-by-step close** avoids asking for a decision, and instead asks for opinions about several components *of* the decision. If the other person is timid, the process can be accompanied by frequent reminders that *no decision is being made about the larger issue*—only systematic statements of preference. At the end, of course, the decision has actually been made, so you can end with a subtle request for agreement.

The **Assumptive close**—long the favorite of automobile dealers—simply acts as if the decision has been made. You say something like, "Great! I'm glad that's settled! So, let's get started—Sandy you can do so-and-so; Kelly, you can do such-and-such, and I'll handle the thingies." In more complicated situations, you might ask for an "OK" or an "Authorization" or an "Approval" in the form of initials on a memo.

Trickiest, most elegant, and hardest of all to execute properly is the **Positive Negative close**. It requires accurate and complete PK_1 and PK_2 knowledge, because it consists of *reminding the other person of something negative about the proposal that you know is unimportant, irrelevant, or even undesirable to him or her*. When you give this "warning," the other person may *correct you*, explain or affirm his or her needs, and thereby *talk himself or herself into the decision you want to achieve*. This works especially well with people equipped with a strong ego.

When you compare the five types of close to the four major types of decision-making style, it quickly becomes obvious that there are some good matches, and some probable danger signs.

Probable **good** closing (and general communication) choices for each of the social styles are as follows:

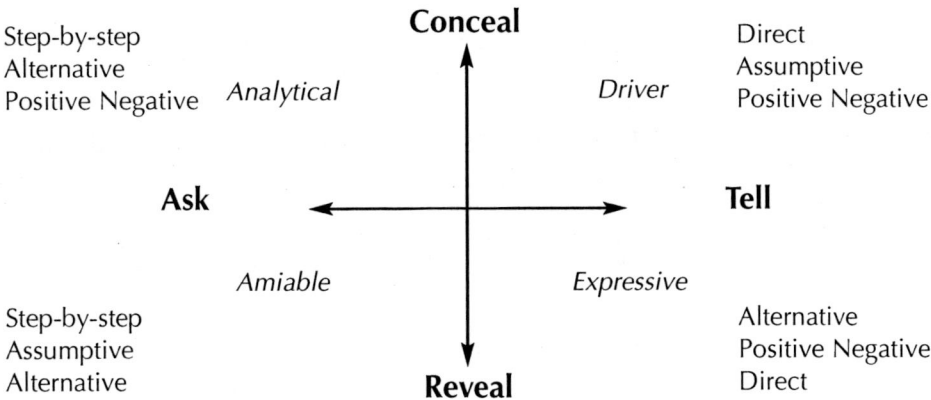

Step-by-step
Alternative
Positive Negative   *Analytical*

Conceal

Driver

Direct
Assumptive
Positive Negative

Ask   **Tell**

Amiable   *Expressive*

Step-by-step
Assumptive
Alternative

Reveal

Alternative
Positive Negative
Direct

Some obvious things to **avoid** would include

Never use a Step-by-step close with a Driver,
Never use a Positive Negative close with an Amiable, and
Never use a Direct close with an Amiable or an Analytical.

This tool allows you to increase your successful "closes"—your achievement of effective persuasive communication—dramatically. It may seem to require a lot of work, but in reality practiced users of this system can position another person in the five main decision-making areas in under 2 minutes, by asking two SHE questions establishing

- The amount of information provided in response,
- The relevance of that information to the question asked,
- The eye motion and words used to show channel usage,
- The sibling positioning of the other person,
- Whether that person is a teller or an asker, and
- Whether that person is a concealer or a revealer—

and from that, the communications plan establishes itself.

Chapter 12
Action Activity

You can learn these skills, if you practice. These exercises can get you started; also, every day try to identify a couple of people—strangers, ideally, since that will force you to be practical—as a discipline.

General Activity

Consider the people with whom you normally work, or other people with whom you can practice. Ask yourself the two questions about each:

Compared to others, this person falls where indicated on the continuum of "concealing" to "revealing" personal information:

CONCEALS	REVEALS
SELF	SELF

"Average"

Compared to others, this person falls where indicated on the continuum of first "asking" or "telling" what to do:

ASK TO	TELL TO
EXPRESS	EXPRESS

"Average"

Then, using this grid, determine each person's social/decision-making style, and select a suitable closing method for each person:

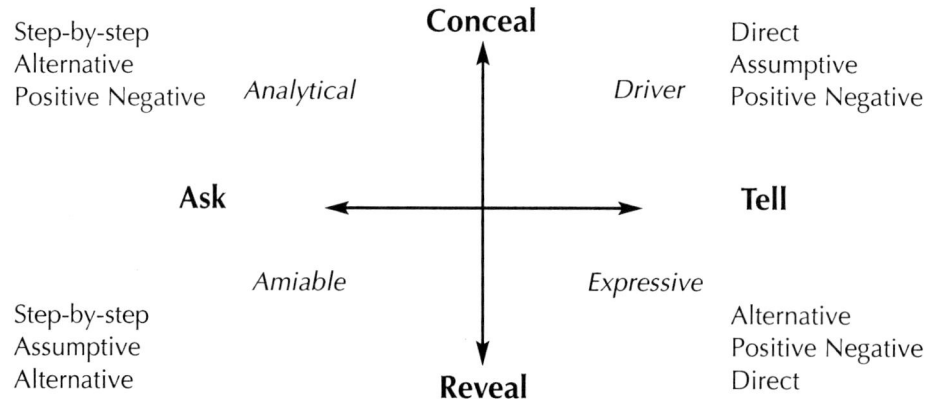

CLOSING METHODS   *CLOSING METHODS*

Step-by-step
Alternative
Positive Negative   *Analytical*   *Driver*   Direct
                                                     Assumptive
                                                     Positive Negative

Ask ← → **Tell**

Amiable   *Expressive*

Step-by-step   Alternative
Assumptive   Positive Negative
Alternative   Direct

Conceal / **Reveal**

The social/decision making style of the people with whom I work, and the "closing" method I would use with each person, are as follows:

	His/her primary communication channel	*Secondary communication channel, if any.*
Each person, by name:		
1. _____	_____	_____
2. _____	_____	_____
3. _____	_____	_____
4. _____	_____	_____
5. _____	_____	_____
6. _____	_____	_____
7. _____	_____	_____
8. _____	_____	_____
9. _____	_____	_____
10. _____	_____	_____

Specific Activity

Applying these skills to the real world in which you live day-to-day, and specifically applying them to a specific project involving actual people, begins by asking one or more SHE questions for instant (and on-going) personal analysis. An effective SHE question will allow you to

- Test *eye motion* and listen to the type of vocabulary used (to determine the **information acquisition** channel in use)
- Measure the *richness and complexity of the content* (to discover the person's **information processing** and **information-provision** styles, and
- Establish the parameters of the *communication values* (to decide on his or her **social/decision making** styles, and from that select an appropriate *close.*

And, obviously, doing this will require that you have ready at hand several SHE questions, so you don't have to be fumbling around in your mind writing one and focusing on yourself instead of on the other person. Now would be a great time to start building this vocabulary of SHE questions, so you can use the skills in this and the foregoing chapters.

Remember, the letters SHE stand for **S**pecific, **H**istoric and **E**vent. The SHE question must be designed to make the other person pause to *remember* something, not have to imagine or develop an idea. Similarly, the other person must not have to remember something *difficult* or *impersonal*—the memory must be casual but meaningful. And—perhaps hardest of all to remember—it must not *lead the answer's form by the specifics it requests.* That is, your question must not ask specifically for a picture, or a feeling, or a sound, since that would direct the answer to a specific channel—usually the *asker's*, rather than the answerer's. In other words, you **wouldn't** ask someone questions such as

- "What kind of look do you want for this project?" *(This is a question about the future, not the past, requiring imagination rather than memory.)*
- "What did your first car look like?" *(This will automatically get a* Visual *reply, since it asks for a specific* picture. *All you know is that the questioner is a Visual.)*
- "Who was the Vice-President under Lyndon Johnson?" *(This is both specific and impersonal, as well as sounding like a question from a school exam.)*

In this space, please write three effective SHE questions *that you would be comfortable using*—that is, the questions must not be more outgoing or personal than you yourself think you could use in a real world situation. Here are examples of a few good SHE questions:

- "What is there about your current office that you would like to have in your new project?"
- "Can you describe a recent project you've encountered that has some features that you really dislike?"
- "What do you remember about your first house (or "car," "office," "building," "spouse," whatever).

Please write three SHE questions *you* like here:

1._____

_____

_____

2._____

_____

_____

3._____

_____

_____

Is each of these a question about a Specific Historic Event? Can you imagine yourself using them? If not, please improve before proceeding!

Specific Activity, cont'd.

It is also essential to remember that *it is very rare for someone to be an **extreme** social or decision-making style.* Most people are *combinations* of styles, so they can be thought of as "Expressive Drivers," or "Driving Amiables," or the like. (Notice that in English the adjective—the *lesser* quality—comes *first*, and the noun—the *major* quality—comes second.) As you get to know people, you will find they go in one or another "corner" of the quadrants in which they fall, so that (for example) someone in the *upper left corner* of the "Driver" quadrant is an *Analytical* Driver, someone in the *lower left corner* pf the same quadrant is an *Amiable* Driver, someone in the *lower right corner* is an *Expressive* Driver, and someone in the upper right corner is a *Driving Driver*—a very rare animal, indeed. The same is true of the other three quadrants, of course.

Knowing what you know, and using as a model the upcoming project that requires the cooperation of other people, continue your evaluation practice by listing those people, your best guess about their social/decision-making styles, and the closing method to use for each person here. Try to fine-tune your evaluation of the decision-making styles, using the continua to spot the *corners* of people's quadrants:

The project: _____

The people with whom I shall be working on this project:	*Each person's social/ decision-making style, as an adjective/noun:*	*The best closing method for use with this person:*	
1. _____	_____	_____	_____
2. _____	_____	_____	_____
3. _____	_____	_____	_____
4. _____	_____	_____	_____
5. _____	_____	_____	_____
6. _____	_____	_____	_____
7. _____	_____	_____	_____
8. _____	_____	_____	_____
9. _____	_____	_____	_____
10. _____	_____	_____	_____

Decision-Making Styles Reference

As with the Information Processing Styles Checklist (see Chapter 7), there have been requests for a summary "cheat sheet" for using the tools of this analytical method with real-world people. This is on the next page; however, the same reminders apply here as before:

- ***First,** use this with the proFILE™ (at the back of the book) so you can organize your observations and ideas for dealing with another person. (Incidentally, most people are flattered to learn that you are taking the time to accommodate their personal needs and desires. The very act of completing the proFILE™ improves relations. Proof? Read on!*

- ***Second,** research has clearly shown that when people perceive that their needs are being respected, their receptivity improves automatically. One simple example: when researchers gave three groups of people with identical horoscopes, but presented the horoscopes differently, the individuals had markedly different responses. People who were given the horoscopes without any preparation at all thought they were mildly interesting; people who were asked their birth dates before being given the horoscopes thought the analyses were fairly accurate, and people who were asked for specifics about their births thought the readings were surprisingly perceptive. And these were identical horoscopes, remember—only the recipient's perceptions of relevance were different.*

- ***Third,** as noted in Chapter 7, remember that you must use these tools only to honor and respect other people by accommodating their communications preferences and requirements. Your goal is improved relationships, not manipulation (in the bad sense). You are learning how to "do unto other people as they would like to be done by."*

- ***Fourth,** remember also that Cartesian Coördinates allow for variations and subtleties in methods and perceptions. Be aware of the subtypes of each person with whom you work.*

- ***Finally,** remember to match, not model the other person, without violating your own integrity in the process. Find ways of meeting the other person on some common ground you honestly share. With that—Have fun!*

The Communication Styles Grid

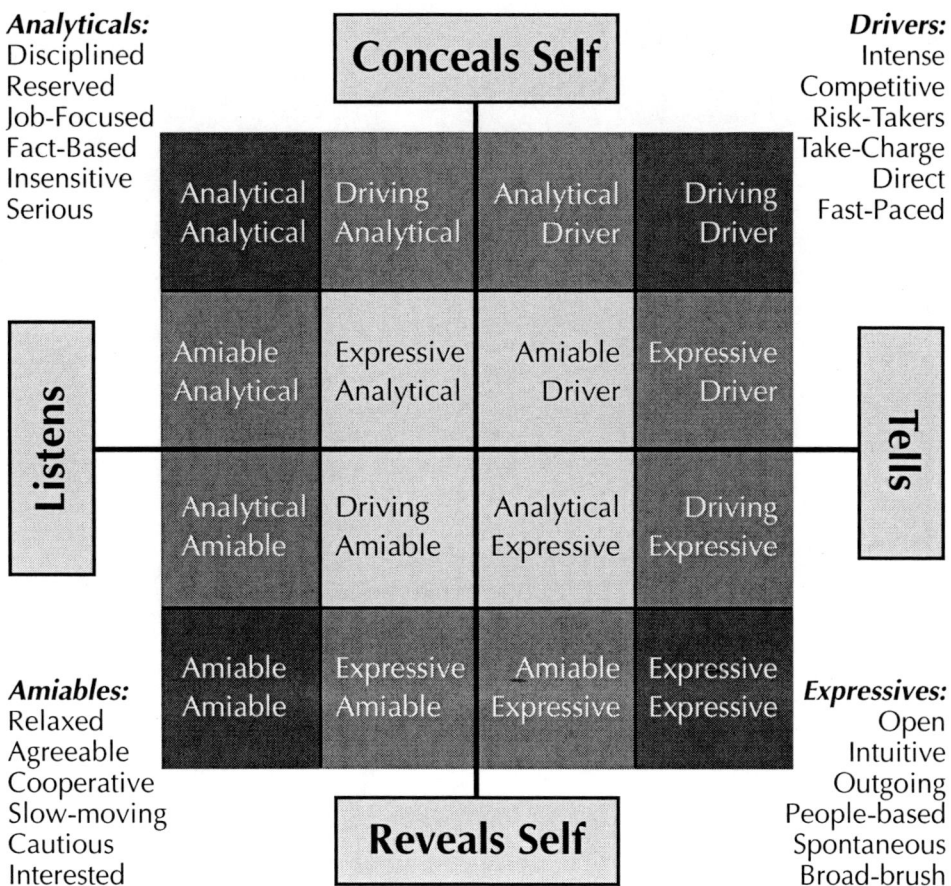

Analyticals:
Disciplined
Reserved
Job-Focused
Fact-Based
Insensitive
Serious

Drivers:
Intense
Competitive
Risk-Takers
Take-Charge
Direct
Fast-Paced

Conceals Self

Analytical Analytical	Driving Analytical	Analytical Driver	Driving Driver
Amiable Analytical	Expressive Analytical	Amiable Driver	Expressive Driver
Analytical Amiable	Driving Amiable	Analytical Expressive	Driving Expressive
Amiable Amiable	Expressive Amiable	Amiable Expressive	Expressive Expressive

Listens

Tells

Reveals Self

Amiables:
Relaxed
Agreeable
Cooperative
Slow-moving
Cautious
Interested

Expressives:
Open
Intuitive
Outgoing
People-based
Spontaneous
Broad-brush

Most of the communication styles you will encounter are clustered around the center of the grid. Subtle differences are important. To identify channels, look for answers to the two questions:

Do people reveal their own feelings or not (SELF)?

Do they talk or listen when making decisions (WILL)?

Now: What will you do with this?

Content:	*What do you want to accomplish?*
Conforming:	*How should you communicate?*
Contact:	*What face-to-face skills will work?*
Control:	*How will you handle circumstances?*
Continue:	*How will you leverage this success?*

Do unto others as they would be done by.

"The Englishman's strong point is his vigorous insularity; that of the American his power of adaptation. Each of these attitudes has its perils. The Englishman stands firmly on his feet, but he who merely does this never advances. The American's disposition is to step forward even at the risk of a fall."

—Thomas Wentworth Higginson

CHAPTER 13: PERSUASION, STEP 5:

▲   HANDLING EMOTIONAL OBSTACLES   ▲
AND USING NEGOTIATION STRATEGIES

"If ignorance were bliss, more people would be happy."

—Gerry Poster,
after Philip Howard

CHAPTER 13: PERSUASION, STEP 5
▲ WHAT TO DO WHEN THE ANSWER IS "NO" ▲

If there is anything people don't want when conducting a persuasive conversation, it is for all their efforts—which seem so very reasonable, now that they have been couched in proper communication styles—to fail. Yet failure is always an option (despite the vainglorious boastings of various self-appointed business gurus); preparing for it, so that an acceptable outcome can be wrested from the jaws of defeat, is the mark of an intelligent (and more-likely-to-be-successful-in-the-long-run) persuasive communicator.

The first decision the persuader must make—and this should be done before the conversation even starts—is articulating clearly the options that would be acceptable outcomes. They might include giving more than originally desired for his or her side of the bargain, settling for a lesser product, or finding another, less-convenient supplier. But—and this is the critical step—*the negotiator must always begin the conversation with a clear and unqualified sense of how much is too much, too late, or too little.* Failure to do this, allowing the negotiations to continue to the point that real boundaries have been broken, will result in a true disaster: having what you want, but having paid too great a price for it.

That having been said, the next step is preparing for the obstacles that might actually occur in the conversation. The first step is realizing that the word "No" covers a lot of ground, and it's not all alike. For example, sometimes the word "No" doesn't mean "No"—it merely can mean "**Not** now," "**Not** like this," or, possibly (and personally painfully), "**Not** you." And *these replies actually are the next best thing to a "Yes," because they mean that the conversation is still active, and your partner wants to get to the desired conclusion. However, obstacles remain—and you must identify and eliminate or minimize them.*

You can quickly identify the obstacles once you clarify whether your partner is saying "**Not** now," or "**Not** you." "**Not** you" means that the remaining obstacles are *emotional*, while "**Not** now" means they have to do with *content*. An emotional obstacle is *personal*; it has to do with how people *feel* about the *terms* of the conversation. A content obstacle is fact-based; it has to do with *characteristics* of the thing being discussed.

Emotional obstacles are dealt with by establishing rapport; the skills you've been learning in this book help you do that. However, if you've gotten to the end of the conversation and the emotional obstacles remain, the skills haven't worked for you, and there's no reason to think they'll work any better if you use them again. It's time to turn the conversation over to someone else. It is better for someone else to have a victory than for you to have a defeat.

Content obstacles are more interesting. There are five types:
- **Not** interested: the condition of *indifference*
- **Not** informed: *misunderstanding* an important fact.
- **Not** convinced: *Skepticism* about a claim or promise.
- **Not** satisfied: Discovery of a real *perceived drawback*
- **Not** enough: Having remaining *unmet expectations*.

Handling content obstacles is much easier than it might look at first. There are five specific strategies to be used, for each of the five types of content obstacle. The five *strategies* are as follows:
- For *Indifference*: Use open probes to uncover unrealized needs.
- For *Misunderstanding*: Provide "but-free" clarification
- For *Skepticism*: Offer appropriate proof, *in the appropriate way.*
- For *Perceived drawbacks*: Introduce offsetting benefits.
- For *Unsatisfied demands*: Employ Win/win negotiation

Let's consider these in greater detail.

Handling indifference. Indifference is easy. All you are dealing with is inadequate preparation on your part, and lack of understanding of your partner's needs; therefore, you simply probe to discover other needs which can be satisfied with benefits of the features of your proposal. Obviously, the preferred technique would be *open* probes, since these gather information most quickly; if this proved inadequate—and it might, because the indifferent partner has little reason to be interested in your subject, by definition—be prepared to shift to *closed* probes.

Handling misunderstandings. Misunderstandings are only slightly harder to handle than indifference. You must provide correct information, but you can't simply correct the other person. That would come across as patronizing at best, and insulting at worst. It suggests that you are smarter or better-informed than the other person that—even if it is true—will do nothing to advance your relationship. A typical correction sounds like this: "Oh—you thought the delivery date was Thursday. It's really Wednesday." Unspoken, but present in the air, is the continuation—"you dope." You can prevent this if you watch your tone of voice carefully (always a good idea anyhow), but there still is a risk of failure.

Another solution, used by many people, is to make a statement that begins with a compliment or other positive statement. It sounds like this: "I can see why you would want to get that as you described. You've made a great case for this position. But let me show you another approach." Again, the person feels insulted—and, in this case, you've made it even easier for them to get their feelings hurt, because you helpfully pointed out the evidence of your superior intelligence by preceding it with the word "But."

There is a third approach, and it's by far the best of all. It's called the "But-free correction." It is a simple trick, no more—but it is an excellent trick. It goes like this:

Whenever you correct someone, or provide a qualification of any kind, do so without the word "but." Use the word "and" instead. This will require that you revise the sentence slightly, and this may require that you change how you think; that's good. That's the idea. That, in fact, is the trick that makes the whole thing work.

Consider why it works: we have been conditioned to recognize that the word "but" signals the real meat of a sentence. For example, if you say to me, "Gerry, I really enjoyed reading *Natural Feelings, Unnatural Acts,* but I think you should have used more examples," you and I both know that what you're telling me is "Revise the book with more examples." And—to add insult to injury—we also know that the subtext of your sentence continues like this: "If you make the change, I'll like your book better, *because it will be more like I would have done it—and, after all, I am MIBU."*

On the other hand, simply revising the sentence by replacing the "but" with an "and" greatly shifts the focus. Now it becomes, "Gerry, I really enjoyed reading *Natural Feelings, Unnatural Acts,* and the examples were my favorite part. I sure hope you'll include even more in the next edition." That sentence tells me that *you liked the book, recognized something good in it, and care enough about __me__ as MIBU to encourage me to do more of what I was doing.* That's a very different—and much more palatable, and relationship-building, message.

Another example: compare these two sentences: **Version 1:** "This is a small house, **but** it has a great view." *Translation:* "This house is uncomfortable, so look out the window and it won't seem so bad." **Version 2:** "This is a small house, **and** it has a great view." *Translation:* "This house is easy to maintain, in addition to having a great location."

Eliminate buts. You will be happier, and so will your partners in communication.

Handling skepticism. Skepticism is another tricky one; like misunderstandings, they tread on the edge of rudeness. But here the liability is shifted: it is your *partner* who skirts danger, because doubting your word holds great potential for an insult. Resolving the problem requires, first, that you *not accept* the burden of the insult, and then, second, *accept* the talk of eliminating the source of doubt by offering *appropriate* proof, *in the appropriate way.*

The "appropriate" way in each case is determined, obviously, by the other person's *communications channel* and *decision-making style* requirements. Your proof for a Driving Visual will be *entirely* different in form and style from the *same* piece of evidence provided to an Amiable Audial.

The form of a proof statement is simple: repeat your initial claim in a calm and nonconfrontational—enthusiastic, if you can manage it—way, offer your proof, and then ask a Closed Probe to verify your success. Repeat until done.

Handling perceived drawbacks. Perceived drawbacks are real, honest-to-God flaws in your proposal that your partner has astutely discovered. There is only one way of handling this: introduce offsetting benefits to compensate for the liability. You do this, of course, with closed probes; this requires your mastery of PK_1 features, so you can provide them as *benefits* that matter to that PK_2 person, using the PK_3 skills of asking the *Closed Probe* (to which you know the answer will be "Yes,") and then making powerful *Support Statements*. Think of this process as a sort of extended "Step-by-step" Close; you ask for agreement about all the smaller items on the list—adding more if need be; see the next Problem—and when you get to the end, you ask whether this was enough to tip the scales. Surprisingly often, it is; the other person's *real* need may simply have been for more time or attention.

Handling unsatisfied demands. An unsatisfied demand is much like indifference; it exposes poor initial probing. The solution, therefore, lies with further probing, to uncover further hidden needs; the best—indeed, usually the *only*—tool to use is a complex probing strategy. As usual, try Open Probes first (since they are more efficient); however, be sensitive to the possibility that your lack of useful understanding may be the result of overly-casual probing, and that a careful, precise *closed probe* strategy is now required. Once you have found a Need, you can set about the real work: again, you provide PK_1 features, as *benefits* that matter to that PK_2 person, using the PK_3 skills of making powerful *Support Statements*.

These are some of the most "unnatural acts" in this book. But they can help you wrest disaster from the jaws of defeat: they have done so many times, for countless millions of people.

Win/win negotiation.

Finally, there is what to do when a logical blank wall has been uncovered—when the two parties have worked together, and they cannot overcome an insurmountable barrier. When this happens, the last step before failure is negotiation.

But (and the word is used here advisedly) negotiation carries a heavy price. Negotiation results in neither party having what s/he desired, and always wondering if s/he could have gotten more. The classic example is the purchase of a car, in which the seller and buyer negotiated back and forth over price—both always wonder if they really had reached the other person's final position. This is bad in a "temporary" event, such as a once-every-four-years purchase; it can be devastating in a long-term relationship, such as in a family or business.

There is a way of minimizing the damage, and it offers other benefits as well. It is called "Win-win negotiation," and is based on the old premise, "If everyone wants a larger slice of the pie, let's get a larger pie." In other words, change the rules, and you can change the outcome. Let's see how this works.

There are seven rules for effective win/win negotiations. All require work.

The first rule is ***never enter a negotiation without a clear sense of what you want, what your non-negotiable limits are, and what you will accept as alternatives for what you desire.*** You began this process back in the Goal-Setting of Step 6; this is where you put it to use.

The second rule is ***prioritize expectations and desires***. Not all of the things on your goal list are of equal importance; make certain that you know the "A" issues from the "C" ones so you can get what you want in a realistic way: for example, do you really want a Lincoln, or do you merely want a luxury car, or do you want an American car? Of those three desires, one must be more important than the others; know that going in.

Third, realize that your partner has needs and desires, too, and they probably aren't as well articulated as yours. If you ***take the time to help the other person articulate wants and prioritize them***, you will not only accelerate and improve the negotiation process—you'll probably make a friend at the same time.

Fourth, remember that your goal is not defeating the other person—it's achieving whatever your purpose was*. Therefore, always try to **give and get, so both sides can feel victorious**. This will build relationships. Doing this requires your having prioritized SPAM goals, of course; as you compare your goals to the other person's you can find ways of giving something in return for what you want, or asking for something that will make you gift more acceptable. And remember—we are talking about *adding* to the deal, not subtracting from it. Subtraction is called *compromise*, about which, please see below.

Fifth, a very important PK3 skill is simply **avoiding the words "I" and "you"—instead, use the first person plural ("We") whenever possible**. This sets the tone for the conversation, and the future.

Sixth—and this sounds strange—**avoid compromise**. A compromise is a lessening of yourself and your position, which usually means at the end you (and, often, the other person as well) will come up short. For example, if you want to leave at 6:00, and the person who must relieve you doesn't want to come in until 7:00, compromising means coming in at 6:30, which means both of you will be unhappy. "Give and get" means you say, "OK, suppose if you come in at 6:00, and tomorrow I'll stay until 8:00. That will give both of us time to make our plans. Would that work for you?" Don't cut the pie differently; instead, keep trying to find ways to change its size, consistency, or filling.

Finally, **know when to hold and when to fold.** Some requirements are non-negotiable, and others can be accommodated only if other concessions are made. For example, if you are keeping kosher, no amount of price reductions will compensate for beef that has been cooked in lard. If you are purchasing Christmas gifts, a delivery date after 25 December isn't acceptable. If you have $100 cash in your pocket, $200 cash right now is more than you can spend, even if it would buy a new Mercedes-Benz. If you don't accept and understand this, you condemn yourself either to certain disappointment or, equally bad, a lifetime of "I might have's"; with understanding and SPAM goals, you can be as happy as possible in the circumstances of life as they unfold.

This merely scratches the surface of this tool, of course—but it's a pretty deep scratch. If you practice these skills—and do the preparatory exercises in this book that give them meaning—they will serve you well.

(If your goal is defeating other people, the present writer requests that you not ever read this book again.)

Chapter 13
Action Activity

These steps are very hard. Good luck.

General Activity

There are many things that you want and desire in life. Some are goals, and can be described in SPAM terms; some are values, and can only be named. (A semi-SPAM *goal* might be *"Retire to Florida in 10 years with an income of $150,000 per year"*; a *value* might be *"Good reputation," "God," "My family's happiness,"* or the like. To prevent future unhappiness, take a piece of paper (such as the one following) and list all the things you want or care about. Put them in columns. Then rank the items in each column from "1" (the most important) down. There will be a "1" in each column, but only *one* "1" in each column. Convert the items in the "Goals" column into SPAM format and double check your rankings. That's you.

GOALS   VALUES

_____   _____

_____   _____

_____   _____

_____   _____

_____   _____

_____   _____

_____   _____

_____   _____

_____   _____

_____   _____

_____   _____

_____   _____

_____   _____

_____   _____

_____   _____

Specific Activity

With candor and honesty, reflect upon your anticipated negotiation. Answer questions such as the following (there are others, relevant to your particular circumstance, which will need to be added. For example—

- Is there a limit to what your dignity will tolerate?
- Are there religious or other requirements that must be met?
- What is the most you will pay?
- What is the least you will accept?
- What is the latest delivery date you can tolerate?

Record those limitations here (you will want to return to the Step 6 Action Activity for reference). Then **rank them from most to least important, <u>circle</u> any that are nonnegotiable. Make sure you like the list.**

When you finish, please turn the page. There, you can start the next stage of your PK$_2$ work, developing lists **based on the probable desires of the other person in this communication process**.

_____

_____

_____

_____

_____

_____

_____

_____

_____

_____

_____

_____

_____

_____

_____

_____

_____

_____

Possible goals of the other person in this persuasive exchange:

_____

_____

_____

_____

_____

_____

Possible WIIFMS for the other person that I could add to the mix if necessary:

_____

_____

_____

_____

_____

_____

Possible nonnegotiables for the other person:

_____

_____

_____

_____

_____

_____

My biggest concerns about this persuasive communication at this point, and how I plan to overcome them:

_____

_____

_____

_____

_____

_____

What is the likelihood of my encountering *indifference?*

_____

If I do, what shall I do about it? (Refer to the previous page for help.)

_____

_____

_____

What is the likelihood of my encountering *misunderstanding?*

_____

If high, revise your plan.

What is the likelihood of my encountering *skepticism?*

_____

If high, what proofs do you have? Are they in the correct communications channel for this person? (Refer to Step 4 and 10.)

_____

_____

_____

What is the likelihood of my encountering *perceived drawbacks?*

_____

If high, am I prepared? (Refer to the previous page for help.)

_____

_____

_____

CHAPTER 14:
▲   IMPLEMENTATION AND APPLICATION   ▲

"The truth is more important than the facts."

—Frank Lloyd Wright

Obviously, this little book contains a great deal of information in a very small space; equally obviously, that means that unless you participated in a seminar to fill in the gaps—or even if you *did* participate in a seminar, but enough time has elapsed to make some of the points a little hard to remember or put into practice—this may seem a lot to take in at once

And the simple fact is that this *is* too much information to take in at once; in fact, just as proper **presentation** of these ideas, including enough time to practice them so the skills become your own, takes forty contact hours and many, many exercises and small-group activities so proper **application** (which means internalizing and employing) them can take weeks, months or longer. Even then, not everyone becomes fully comfortable with *all* the methods and tools, and must pick and choose from among them just to begin improving.

Those facts should serve both as **encouragement** and **caution** for anyone desiring to use these materials and ideas to become a more effective persuasive communicator. Luckily, there are four *different* ways you can set about learning these skills. Here they are.

Approach 1:
The Organic Method

Reflect over the content of this book and recognize that you like some parts of it more than others. That's OK, you're MIBU, remember, and things matter to the degree that you want them to matter. (However, also be aware that *different* MIBUS like *different* parts of the book; the differences are in the readers, rather than in the applicability, usefulness, or accuracy of the content.)

Now that you have admitted you have preferences, go through the book chapter-by-chapter and highlight the topics you particularly like. (Don't mark the stuff you dislike; that may change over time.) Then pick *one*—just *one*—of the tools or skills, and resolve to make it your own. Commit to mastering that skill, and employ it every day. The present author recommends either *Support Statements* or *Information Acquisition Channels* (Chapters 3 and 4, respectively) if nothing else jumps out at you; these are sound foundations for your growth.

Practice these skills for a couple of weeks, or even a month or so. Reread the sections in this book, and reread them again. Ask questions of yourself, and keep practicing. Do it until they have become second nature. Then go to another skill, and do the same.

In this manner, you will master all the skills of an effective persuasive communicator. It may take you half a year or so; that's OK, if you've got the time. If you don't—you can move faster, if you wish.

Approach 2:
The Behavorial Method

Another way to learn these skills is to develop a simple set of behaviors for your persuasive communications contacts. Here is one such set, discussed more fully in the MAST seminar *Herding Cats for Fun and Profit.*

Rule 1: Plan a meeting. Make certain that you clearly understand the goal of your persuasive communications before you start. Once you have accomplished your goal, verify that you have a reason for returning to this contact person and then end the meeting. You are a *guest;* don't overstay your welcome. You are a *professional;* don't go in without a purpose.

Rule 2: Match the other person whenever possible. If she is speaking softly, speak softly. If he is nervous, act nervous. If she touches your arm, touch her arm. The customer is the judge of what is right; to the degree that you can validate that without compromising your own values and comfort level, do so.

Rule 3: As much as possible in the context of Rule 1, be positive. Nod when you make a point. Make your voice exude confidence; end your sentences firmly and with strength. Stand up and smile when you're on the phone with a customer. Listen to yourself on a tape recording and ask if you would like to associate with someone who sounds like that.

Rule 3: Watch out for barriers. Natural obstacles exist everywhere, and it's all too easy to use them as defensive shields. Conference tables, for example: don't let them "come between" (notice the phrase?) yourself and the other person. Instead, move around to the side on which they are standing, and work together on finding a solution or selecting a product—"Come together," as John Lennon would put it.

Rule 5: Be sensitive to other people's needs for proofs and documentation. Review Chapter 11; be very sensitive to requests for documentation *or the lack thereof.* The *format in which you provide that proof* is determined by the other person's communications channel. As noted before, in other words,
  • For a visual, offer proof in the form of written testimonials, warranties, pictures of installations, well-lighted samples held at arm's length for examination, and so on. Use your body as an easel.

• For an audial, offer proof in the form of stories and narratives, offering the phone numbers of people to call for testimonials, anecdotes of others' experiences, and so on. Use your body as a verbal clearing-house.

• For experientials, have samples ready for mauling, take the person to places to check things out, and give them things to do to become involved with the product and you. Make certain to go out of your way for them, and make sure they know you do it. Use your body as a workhorse.

Approach 3:
The "Just Do It" Method

This is a variation on the "Behavioral Method" mentioned above. There, you build a learning schedule for the skills in this book around a one-on-one meeting with another person. This allows you to concentrate on the "direct" persuasive communication skills, such as matching, positioning, and structuring. In the "Just Do It" method you plan a formal meeting or presentation to a group (of any size), so that you force yourself to implement skills in structuring and planning, rather than by reacting and responding. This method is both **safer** (since it allows you to anticipate situations rather than handling them) and more **risky** (since it exposes you to a wider variety of people and possibilities). Here's how it works.

(Incidentally, you might want to attend the *Koloman, Samson and Balaam's Ass* Seminar—or at least read the book—before using this method. It will make things much easier for you.)

First, decide what you will present (a proposal or recommendation, which is your *product*), and the customers to whom you will speak. These can be **internal** (Associates whom you must influence), **external** (people to whom you wish to sell something) or any other type.

Then establish a plan for the meeting. As you plan, you should consider the various ideas you learned from this book, and the implications and ramifications of the system. Specifically, you must decide (based on analysis and evidence, not assumption and *self*-projection) what are likely to be your Customers' expectations, needs and desires in each of the following areas (see the *pro*FILE, in the Action Assignments, for help with this):
  • What are the probable **psychological needs** motivating the other people in their consideration of your proposal—that is, where arc they on Maslow's Hierarchy?
  • How do these people **communicate** with you, and with each other? Should you plan to ask questions or make statements—that is, should you employ a probing/supporting strategy, and if so what sort of probes should you use (open or closed)?

- How will you cover off all seven possible information acquisition needs of the people in the audience—the three types of Visual and the two types of each of Audial and Experiential? (Again, use the sheet on page 125 to test your own preferences against those of other people. You are MIBU, but so are they.)
- How will you accommodate the four **thinking styles** (Soldier, Doctor, Minister, Police Officer?
- How will you accommodate the four **social/decision-making styles** (Driver, Analytical, Amiable, and Expressive) *and what sort of close(s) will you use with this group, based at least in part upon your analysis of*
- Whatever are the existing internal authority relationships of the group (remember, to a greater or lesser degree they have worked out some sort of *détente* before they reached your shores, and you must appreciate that system), the authority and proof needs of the real (functional rather than titular) decision-maker, and your own individual authority expectations and needs? How you can coordinate these various situations for maximum smoothness and minimum unnecessary conflict and friction as you bring things to a mutually satisfactory and beneficial conclusion?

This study—which will not be easy—will guide you through reviewing and applying the critical skills of this book. Thus, you will kill two birds with one stone: you can learn how to make these methods your own, and you can get a real-world success at the same time. Or you could fall flat on your behind—so maybe a fourth method might be a good idea before you decide the best way that you, as an individual, can get your act together and take it on the road.

Approach 4:
The Systematic Method

Finally, so there's another way you can acquire these skills, that seems more dramatic but (in the long run) actually is both simpler and more effective. That is to apply them one-by-one, systematically, to make them part of your life as a whole. The simple logic is that a few basic skills underlie the entire process, and the more you do them, the easier it is. They are:

Asking SHE questions consistently,
Listening for content in the replies, which tell you
 His or her *concerns and needs*
 Holistic/Casuistic attitudes
 Interpersonal relationships, for *tell/ask attitudes,* and
 Brevity or loquacity, for *conceal/reveal* preferences.
 Listening for style detail in the replies, including his or her
 Cooperation/openness, which tells you how to probe;

Vocabulary, which tells you the person's then-active communications channel;

Eye motion, which confirms or challenges the communications channel observation, and

Staying-on-point, which reveals linear/associative thought processing styles.

Making Support Statements

Learning how to determine *sibling relationships* politely

Formulating response strategies, and

Making effective requests for commitment—*closes.*

In order to learn these skills, study the content of this book carefully over a 3-month period. Here is a format schedule that you might follow:

Week 1: Review this book, a few pages at a time.

Week 2: Apply Chapter 1. Develop WIIFMs for all your key "products."

Week 3: Apply Maslow to your peers and build models.

Week 4: Continue developing WIIFMs. Begin to make Support Statements whenever possible.

Week 5: Enlist the help of someone you trust to critique your Support Statements. Continue to do practice.

Week 6: Begin probing practice. Consciously shift your style to conform to various circumstances you encounter. Also, develop a "rhythm" for your probing and supporting style. Most conversations should go like this: 1 to 3 "social" or "polite" closed probes, (followed by Support Statements), then 1 to 2 open probes (support each); then use closed probes to direct the conversation to the desired outcome (support each); close.

Week 7: Review Chapters 5 and 11. Begin categorizing people's communication styles and practicing responding to them.

Week 8: Review Chapter 6. Begin practicing how to determine social styles and using the grid.

Week 9: Continue week 8 practice.

Week 10: Apply Chapter 7 and review Chapter 8.

Week 11: Review Chapter 9 and add that information to your peer models.

Week 12: Review and practice applying Chapter 10.

Week 13: Really study Chapter 12. This will require application.

Week 14: Review Chapter 13. (This may take longer than one week.)

A tool that will help you perform this discipline is The *pro*FILE™, a copy of which is in the following Action Activities. You can use this to jog your memory about things to consider; you can actually show your peers the form and fill it in as you ask questions. With other people, you can complete it later, to analyze what you did and did not do—and probably *do not do at the present time.*

Pads of the form, for use in practicing the skills with your real-world associates, are also available.

Notice that the form (please see page 185) has two columns: in the left-hand column, you record your *observations*, based on the responses to your SHE questions. In the right-hand column, you record your *plan in response to the observations*. Thus, if you check "Quiet and reserved" in the left-hand column [a euphemism for "won't talk"], you could write "Use closed probes" in the right-hand column as a note to yourself. If you check "Middle [child]" in the let-hand column, you could write "make deals; offer concessions" in the right, and so on. Then you will have a plan in proceeding with this person in the future.

So, the future of your success as a professional effective persuasive communicator is squarely in your own hands, which is where it was all along. Hopefully, however, by reading this book you have found some ideas

- ***Professed*** that will help you improve
- ***Effectiveness*** (that is, your ability to achieve the goals you desire) by doing a better job of
- ***Persuading*** other people (that is, giving them heart, encouraging and strengthening them) so that you can
- ***Communicate*** with them—that is, help them perceive how you and they are one.

If so, the Present Author will be more than happy—he will be profoundly grateful for your having vivified these concepts, the result of his life's work. And if you have any questions, suggestions or success stories (or anything else), please write:

Gerry Poster
Learning Institute Press
102 West Mountain View Avenue
Greenville, South Carolina 29609-4645

My very best wishes to each reader—

Gerry Poster

Chapter 14
General Action Activity

This section is much shorter than those of the other Action Activities, because the weight of making sense of these skills has shifted from the author's shoulders (where they were carried as they were discovered, developed and tested), to the reader's. If you wish to become a more *effective* persuasive communicator, these ideas and skills must become part of your real-world life, and that means you must now take up this burden and employ it. And it *is* a burden; learning how to understand other people's "natural feelings" is one of the most "unnatural acts" of all.

Accordingly, the first thing you need to do is decide how you want to proceed (if at all). There are five easy and obvious possibilities:

If somehow how have reached this page without agreeing with the ideas in this book—if you reject these methods and don't think they can help you become a happier and more effective person—you should just close the covers and walk away. Actually, you should throw this book down and dance upon it, because you, it, and the author were a bad fit.

If you like one or more of the ideas in this book and prefer the ***"Organic Method,"*** you should develop your priority list of things to do (and not do). For your convenience, here is a check list that can serve as a planning outline:

Like a lot	Like a little	Neutral about	Idea	Do now	Do soon	Do later
☐	☐	☐	Features and Benefits	☐	☐	☐
☐	☐	☐	Maslow's Hierarchy	☐	☐	☐
☐	☐	☐	Open/Closed Probes	☐	☐	☐
☐	☐	☐	Support Statements	☐	☐	☐
☐	☐	☐	Projection techniques	☐	☐	☐
☐	☐	☐	Seers/hearers/doers	☐	☐	☐
☐	☐	☐	Processing styles	☐	☐	☐
☐	☐	☐	Goal-settings	☐	☐	☐
☐	☐	☐	Attitude handling: SET	☐	☐	☐
☐	☐	☐	Authority relationships	☐	☐	☐
☐	☐	☐	Analyzing eye motion	☐	☐	☐
☐	☐	☐	Decision-making styles	☐	☐	☐
☐	☐	☐	Negotiation strategies	☐	☐	☐

If you prefer one of the other methods of implementing these ideas, please continue reading this activity.

If you like the **"Behavioral Method,"** you need to make a few simple decisions, as follows:

- Who will be your primary contact (and with whom will you continue your exercise, after this first experience)?

    Name: _____

- When and where will this take place?

    Commitment: _____

- How will you monitor your progress as the meeting takes place—that is, how can you could measure your success in matching communication styles eliminating barriers, and using proof styles that fit his or her needs "on the fly?"

    *Measurement of progress:*_____

    _____

- How will you measure your total success after the meeting—that is, how will you know whether you succeeded or failed in achieving your stated goal?

    *Measurement of achievement:*_____

    _____

Most important: After the meeting is over, return to this page and evaluate how well you were able to use the skills you learned here in *Natural Feelings, Unnatural Acts.* Specifically, do you know:

- The other person's **Maslow needs?** If not, what will you do to discover them?
- The best **communication style** (open or closed probes) to use with him/her? If not, what will you do to identify it?
- How she or he **acquires information** (visual, audial or experiential)? If not, what will you do to discover this?
- How she or he **processes information** (Doctor, Soldier, Police Officer or Minister)? If not, what will you do to identify it?
- His or her **authority needs,** level of confidence in you, and the role you should maintain? If not, how will you learn it?
- How she or he **makes decisions** (Analytical, Driver, Expressive, Amiable) and how to close him or her? If not, what will you do to discover them?

If you choose to use the ***"Just Do It Method"***—making a formal presentation to real-world Customers in order to learn the skills—you need to plan the presentation. Here is a checklist to help. You also could use the *pro*FILE, which is on page 185; for much more information please see *Koloman, Samson and Balaam's Ass.* At the least you must consider:

- The group's and individual's probably ***psychological needs;***
- Effective ***closed probes*** to use with this group;
- How to accommodate ***information acquisition styles;***
- How to accommodate ***information processing styles;***
- The group's ***social/decision-making style,*** its order of functionality and existing group dynamics and any
- ***Sibling-based authority/trust issues.***

Meeting Planner's Checklist

1. What am I recommending to this group?_____

2. Who is the chief decision-maker? What is his/her social style?

   _____   _____   _____

3. What concerns is this organization facing at this time, and what are their motivations for considering my recommendation? Choose one:
   ☐ Survival   ☐ Security   ☐ Society   ☐ Status   ☐ Self

   What are the probable concerns of the chief decision-maker at this time?
   ☐ Survival   ☐ Security   ☐ Society   ☐ Status   ☐ Self

4. What are the resulting WIIFMs?_____

5. What closed probes can I use to direct them to these WIIFMs?

   _____

   _____

6. How will I accommodate
   Visual learners?   _____

   Audial learners?   _____

   Experiential learners?_____

7. How does this group operate—what are its dynamics?

   ____ _____

   How can I match the authority needs of the decision-maker and group?

   _____

8. How shall I close (request commitment)? _____

Finally, if you like the **"Systematic Method"** (the actual favorite of the Present Author), you need only to set up a schedule. It's pretty easy; just assign "first of the week" dates for the following, all of which relate back to the preceding chapter:

	WEEK BEGINNING:	SUBJECT TO BE MASTERED:	(CHAPTER #)
Week 1	_____	_____	_____
Week 2	_____	_____	_____
Week 3	_____	_____	_____
Week 4	_____	_____	_____
Week 5	_____	_____	_____
Week 6	_____	_____	_____
Week 7	_____	_____	_____
Week 8	_____	_____	_____
Week 9	_____	_____	_____
Week 10	_____	_____	_____
Week 11	_____	_____	_____
Week 12	_____	_____	_____
Week 13	_____	_____	_____
Week 14	_____	_____	_____

Specific Activity

Perhaps the single most important tool in the armory of the effective persuasive communicator is that which makes it *professional* (something that can be verbalized and discussed)—the *pro*FILE. This allows you to analyze each important person in your life so that you can build a face to demonstrate your awareness that she or he is MIBU—someone worthy of your attention and concern.

The form has six sections; if you do not know the answer to an analytical question, you automatically are directed to what you should do next to support the relationship. Complete one form for each person whom you desire to influence, and in some cases—as when one has multiple levels of relationship with another—feel free to complete different forms for the same person based on the specific issues and values at work.

This will repay you many times over, in better relationships, increased mutual satisfaction, and reduced time wastage. Good luck!

*pro*FILE™ v. 4.0

Contact _____

Account _____

UpDATE _____

INFINITE RELATIONSHIPS

PK₂: PERSONAL STYLES	PK₃: PROCESS PLAN

PK₂: PERSONAL STYLES

- **Probable Hierarchical Need**
  (Survival, Security, Society, Status, Self)
  _____

- **Communication Style (Output)**
  - ☐ Easy and open
  - ☐ Talkative and free
  - ☐ Quiet and reserved

- **Information Acquisition Style (Input)**
  - ☐ Visual
  - ☐ Auditory (Hearer)
  - ☐ Experiential (Doer)

- **Usual Information Processing Style**

  Linear (outcome)

  Doctor   Soldier

  Holistic ←———→ **Casuistic**

  Minister   Police Officer

  Associative (process)

- **Dominant Structural Style**
  - ☐ Elder/Eldest/Only *(Challenger)*
  - ☐ Middle *(Collaborator)*
  - ☐ Younger/Youngest *(Columbus)*

- **Usual Decision-Making (Social) Style**

  Conceal

  Analytical   Driver

  Ask ←———→ **Tell**

  Amiable   Expressive

  Reveal

  Modifier _____

  Primary _____

PK₃: PROCESS PLAN

- **How to Address that Need**
  _____
  _____

- **Personal Default Probing Tool:**
  _____ **Probes**

- **Default Presentation Method(s):**
  _____
  _____
  _____

- **Default Processing Plan:**

  His/Her STYLE _____

  Therefore I should:

  Be more _____

  Be less _____

- **Default Relationship:**

  _____ /to/ _____
  (mine)   (his/hers)

- **Default Social Interface:**

  His/Her STYLE _____

  Therefore I should:

  Be more _____

  Be less _____

- **Default Closing Method(s):**
  (Direct, Either/Or, Step-by-Step,
  Assumptive, Postive/Negative)
  _____

NOTES _____
_____

"If God created us in his own image we have more than reciprocated."

—Voltaire

ABOUT THE AUTHOR

Gerry Poster (Gerbrand Poster III), has been an author and trainer for over 30 years. He specializes in communications, problem-solving, persuasion and other forms of selling, team-building, continuous improvement, and diversity cooperation. He has provided training, merchandising, and manufacturing support to the carpet industry for 20 years; he began consulting with Masland's sister companies in 1992, and joined the Dixie Group family in 1995.

Gerry graduated from the University of the South (Sewanee) and Rice University. He served as an officer in the US Navy, and taught at the Naval Academy (Annapolis) and Clemson University before directing his energies to corporate training. He has received subsequent certifications from groups such as Phil Crosby Associates, Learning International, the Forum Group, and similar organizations. He has designed many training programs for individual companies as diverse as optical retailers and auto-industry suppliers.

Gerry prescribes a comprehensive approach to organizational management and development, which is described in his books such as *Trade Secrets: How Successful Leaders Get the Job Done Right the First Time* (about leading continuous improvement), *Natural Feelings, Unnatural Acts (A Professional's Guide to Effective Persuasive Communications)*, *MAST (Masland Applied Sales Training)*, *QP³: Quality People, Quality Processes, Quality Products* (driving continuous improvement into the work force), *The PIG Pack* and *The Bat Book* (hands-on problem-solving tools), *Shibboleths and Shorthand* (an introduction to interior design and architecture), *The Carpet and Rug Handbook,* and *Cat Herding for Fun and Profit*. Masland's clients have direct access to Gerry's help from his offices in South Carolina.

γ ι ν ε σ θ ω ι*

MAKE IT SO!

(Pronounced *ginesthoi*)—ancient Greek for "Make it so"; also, Jean-Luc Picard's command for executing an order in his role as Captain of the Starship *Enterprise* in one of the several *Star Trek* remakes. Once a plan has been developed, all that remains is committing to do the work required to achieve one's goals—to "Make it so."

The above word was found written at the bottom of
a Ptolemaic papyrus that arrived in Alexandria
23 February 33 BC (Mechir 26), probably
written by Cleopatra VII (according to
papyrologist Peter van Minnen at the
University of Groningen in the
Netherlands). This writer hopes
that the Reader will convert
the principles in this
book into assets
for his or her
own life.
▼

Make it so!

(Actually, the word should have been capitalized Γ ιν εσθωι —
but Cleopatra merely spoke Greek as a Second Language.)